Advanced Praise for Peace, Possibilities and Perspective

"Julie is a woman who creates magic in her life. Each chapter of this book is her gift to the reader, offering a window into creating a more intentional and beautiful life. It's a light hearted, and yet very practical guide to being the magician of our own destiny."

–Julie Fedeli, CEO, Entrepreneur, Health & Wellness Expert

"I love the book. It is so inspirational and informative. Your writing style is welcoming and so natural."

–Carlyn Morris, Owner of Back to Wild Adventures

"What struck me is your positive perspective on what at first seemed like serendipitous moments, the development of events by chance in a happy or beneficial way, but what became apparent was that it was something more like resolve. The thread across these is that it is not a matter of chance or luck, which is why the title is 8 secrets -- because everyone can access possibilities with the resolve to do so."

–Dr. Sarah J. Donovan, Assistant Professor of Education

"I loved your book and think you have the most positive and motivated attitude of anyone I've met in a long time. It is so refreshing to hear such positive perspectives, especially in such a scary/unpredictable time like the one we are in right now.

Manifesting is something I have been working on a lot in my personal life. It can be very hard to focus on positivity, but I've had a lot of conversations with friends who are all trying to do the same thing -- I'm a big believer that you receive the energy you put out into the world, and this chapter really hit home for that! I loved the stories and examples.

My favorite line from that chapter was:

"When you get clear, everything else gets clear. Your path becomes apparent. Things you hadn't considered suddenly pop into your mind. And off you go, making it happen."

I think this is a really important message for people to hear right now. I loved reading it and I appreciate all the great energy!"

–Dara Durdic, future lawyer and UCLA grad

"My mind was yelling "*F*ck yeah!*" as you described connecting with the exec at your company. Woot! Woot! Standing at that crossroad of jumping on an opportunity or walking away is totally relatable. I hope your story comes back to me next time I have a choice to go for it.

Your chapter on mindfulness has motivated me to find a quiet space *right now* and start up again. Thanks."

–Paula Beck, Marketing Executive and owner,
Paula Beck Homes

"Loved it!!!!! Really well written and articulated. Regarding manifestation, you did a good job explaining how it works for everybody and your stories are so remarkable.

I got chills reading them."

–Leanne Conlon, Business Owner and Stylist

"I absolutely loved reading your book. I couldn't put it down! I've been divorced for 8 years and have begun getting more and more content living my life alone. However, after reading your book, it makes me want to commit to finding the love of my life. Why settle? The possibilities are endless! I want to exude with such positive energy that people will be drawn to! To start, I plan to begin my days with 3 words of gratitude, filling a gratitude jar and doing 48 acts of kindness! I can commit to that! Nobody holds me back more than myself and that will change starting TODAY! Everything you want, you can have by trusting your dreams."

–Holly Turkington, Human Resource Business Partner

Peace, Possibilities and Perspective

8 Secrets to Serenity and
Satisfaction in Your Life and Career

Julie Bruns

Ignite Press
Fresno, CA

Published in the United States by Ignite Press.
ignitepress.us

ISBN: 978-1-7358081-7-8 (Amazon Print)
ISBN: 978-1-7358081-0-9 (IngramSpark) PAPERBACK
ISBN: 978-1-7358081-1-6 (IngramSpark) HARDCOVER
ISBN: 978-1-7358081-2-3 (E-book)

For bulk purchase and for booking, contact:

Julie Bruns
julie@2possibilityandbeyond.com

Library of Congress Control Number: 2020922006

Content Editing by Tami Mize
Copy Editing by Andrew Hirst
Interior design by Jetlaunch Layout Services
Cover design by Santo Roy

This book is dedicated to every human being that didn't have all the guidance they wanted or needed growing up. To every person that is wondering how they're going to figure out their life and make it in this world: you are not alone. There are people and resources just waiting to help you. Never stop seeking answers. Never stop looking for those great people and leaders. They are out there. You will have everything you need; just don't give up.

Acknowledgements

I would like to thank every person I have encountered on my lifelong journey. No matter what your influence on me, I would not be who I am today without you.

To the three wonderful men I have lived with for half of my life: my husband Brian, and two incredible sons, Jake and Sam. You have taught me more than you'll ever know. My greatest achievement has been creating our family. I am eternally grateful for your support and love all along the way. We are the family I always wished I had.

To my dad, John Merritt Aikman, who spent his life trying to get his dream out into the world and died without making it happen. Every day, I look at the illustration of his unfulfilled dream and remind myself that *I don't have to die* without my dreams coming to fruition. More importantly, I don't want to. Nor do I want that for you.

To every friend I have been blessed with, from childhood until today. You are the constant thread of inspiration, laughter and light that have kept me sane. I don't know where I would be without your constant presence. We should all be so lucky!

Table of Contents

Introduction

When I found out I was pregnant just 5 months after our wedding, I was freaked out. I was 27 years old, just 6 months from finishing my Masters' degree, about to go from *years* of working as a waitress/bartender, working multiple jobs simultaneously, as a full-time student, to *finally* having that regular life, where my husband and I could work normal hours, be off on the weekends, and travel and see friends instead of working while everyone else was enjoying their lives.

"What are we going to do?" I asked my new husband. "We'll figure it out; we **are** married, you know?" Of course, we'll figure it out; we always did. We both came from broken homes. His during pre-adolescence, me in my early 20s, just a few years before we were married. But in my estimation, 10 years too late for my parents. "What are you so worried about?" asked my confused husband. I wasn't sure.

I had a guess. I'd been working since I was 10 years old (babysitting), doing odd jobs to earn spending money and to pay my way through school, as I got good grades, supported myself and figured out how I wanted to spend my life. I was so focused on having the best job, the perfect job, so that I could enjoy my career, because I just **knew** that I had to work. I had to work because it was how

I proved my worth. It never even dawned on me to be financially supported by my husband. I never thought for one second that I could stay at home, so the thought of having a baby was terrifying. I had just spent almost $30,000 and several years earning two college degrees and busting my ass, and now I was going to start my full-time career **and** raise a baby?

As I'm sure you can guess, my husband was less than thrilled with my response to this exciting news. We had just planned and paid for our own wedding with 150 of our family and friends. We were happily married; we knew we had made the right decision and we "chose wisely", as Dr. Laura likes to recommend.

So, what did we do? We figured it out. As always, we made the best of it and we worked hard to do all the right things. That's all we've ever done. Why would this be any different? Well, for starters, I couldn't exactly articulate this at the time, during my shock, but I knew I didn't have a good role model, so how in the hell was I going to *be* a good mom?

Initially, my immediate plan was to finish my degree and keep waitressing until I graduated, then find a good teaching job and we'd figure out the rest. But during my pregnancy, I started substitute teaching and I realized I was not going to make enough money to support a baby and pay for daycare. I can't believe I was even considering this. At the time, in my crazy brain, it wasn't even an option to set aside my education and stay home full-time with my baby. What was I thinking?

I was thinking, "I have to work!" I must earn money; what else is going to make me worthy? What did I do all of this for? Why did I sacrifice for so long, attend college, work 2 jobs, if I'm not going to obtain the job of my dreams? I have spent my life working, or thinking I needed to work, to have value. I have sacrificed my marriage, at times, motherhood, at times, and family relationships because I thought my value in being on the planet was only in actually doing something to earn money, bringing value to others, no matter what the cost. Mostly it was to bring value to people outside my family, to prove I was worthy. I had spent my life thinking that this would bring me happiness, because in the end, I'd prove I was worthy. I finally realized that the proof was never going to come.

I'd spent my life trying to be a better person, so that I could be more worthy. I needed to fix myself so that I could be worthy, and only when I was all fixed up, would I be worthy of having/ getting what I wanted. I also think I did this so that I could help heal my family. If I could find the answers, I could share them with my siblings, and they could be healed. This was a vicious cycle. It was not my job to heal them, though I so deeply wished I could.

And so began my journey of figuring out how to stay happy, peaceful and content, while figuring out just what was possible for my life. I read every book and article I could find, asked a million questions, attended innumerable workshops, did all the work, and was the best I could be at every job I had (including being a mom). And now, I can share my lessons.

I am writing this for every person who knows deep down that the sky's the limit, but doesn't have anyone around them to show them, or anyone who believes in this concept. I'm writing this for people who want to be happy, peaceful, and content in their lives each and every day, AND who also want to have it all, dreaming big dreams and seeing them come true.

I am writing this book for the stressed-out manager who loves their team but cannot find the time to nurture themselves, or the employees they so sincerely know need it. I am writing it for every leader that wishes they could wave a magic wand over people and help them absorb the lessons.

I knew growing up that I would have to figure it all out myself. I have never NOT tried to figure it - or anything - out. This book is my effort to help you figure it out sooner, so that you don't have to wait until your 50th birthday before finally being able to live your dream. Let's help you get there on, maybe, your 30th birthday, okay? And if you're a little late to the game, the secrets in my book are going to show you that, no matter what your age, you **can** get there eventually. Really!

You can read this book one chapter at a time, in order, or you can start in the middle with the chapter that most piques your interest. Either way, when you're done, you will have 8 more tools that can help you feel more peace, see more possibilities, and reflect on your perspective along the way, so that you can live your life in a steady stream of happiness, joy, and contentment.

My secrets illuminate concepts you probably have already considered at some point or simply need to reflect on more because you've had a hint of them along your journey. Consider them guidance and reminders to live your life to its fullest, always wondering what could be. It's those dreams, your dreams, that will change the world.

And for more resources, inspiration, and guidance you can check out my blog, my podcast (The Peace & Possibilities Podcast), or sign up for my newsletter. Let's get you enjoying life!

1

· · · · ·

Possibility

(It is everywhere)

This is how I want you to think about your life and the possibilities that await you: "While it is important to think positively, it is equally important to go beyond positive thinking, and to become aware of the possibilities in every situation, viewing life as more than a struggle to survive, but *an exciting array of challenges and opportunities.*" (http://www.happy-relationships. com/possibility-thinking.html)

Possibility has always been something that fills me with excitement. What could be possible was always in the back of my mind. I remember thinking while I was growing up: What if I could do that? What if I could have that job? What if I could date that boy? What if I could ask that question? What if I could have that life?

Now, today, even just getting on the train to go into the city, whether for work or for fun, is still exciting to me, because I'm always thinking about all of the cool things that **may** happen. As soon as I settle in, get a good seat, and look out the window, I think about all the people on the train, heading to their jobs in their high-rise offices, and I wonder just what the day will bring. I look at the beautiful buildings in the skyline and am grateful that I live in this incredible city. Then I think about all the people that

I will see walking down the street, in the elevator, in the coffee shop, and who I might connect with that day.

I've always been this way. Having something to look forward to has always been important to me. Wondering what was going to unfold has always made my stomach fill with butterflies. And when I'm feeling this way, I sit up a little straighter, pay closer attention, tune into those around me, and notice everything that is going on. Sometimes this is exhausting because I not only notice cool things, I notice people in pain. I've also always been able to sense energy. You know that feeling when you walk into a room and you can feel the tension? Those of you who know what I'm talking about know that this is not always something you welcome. It can be exhausting to be this sensitive and this in tune

> Wondering what was going to unfold has always made my stomach fill with butterflies.

with people. It can be physically draining to know what others are feeling, and not know what to do about any of it. But I digress.

It's also exhilarating, and that's what I choose to focus on. Possibility is exhilarating!

When I think about what is *really* possible, I think about how we are all privileged to be working in this country, or anywhere in the world, to have an office at home or at work, performing everyday tasks using our strengths, and getting paid to use our talents. So, why do some of us settle for something that is just okay? Especially today, when our worlds are much more virtual, and we can do almost anything from our computers or phones… literally, almost anything is actually possible!

To define it more specifically, "If something can happen, it's possible; and if it's possible, it's a possibility!" This quote is from the book: *That's a Possibility!: A Book About What Might Happen…* by Bruce Goldstone. Let me say that again: **If it's possible, it is a possibility**! As we go along in life, we may hear negative feedback about our ideas or dreams, and people may ask, "Do you really think that can happen?" I'm happy to share (like many others that have come before me), that if you can dream it up and create it, then it could **very likely** happen. That's the whole point of life, from my perspective. If you can imagine it, it indeed is a possibility! Let me share a little story to illustrate this.

When I was about 19 years old, I was working two jobs, living with a long-time friend, and saving up money to go back to college. I worked five days a week as a receptionist at an architecture firm in Chicago, and at night I waited tables at a local bar. One day when I was driving home, I heard a commercial on the radio, advertising tryouts for the Chicago Bulls Luvabulls dancers. The tryouts were scheduled for an upcoming Saturday at Ditka's restaurant in Chicago. "Just show up at 8 am on Saturday and be ready to dance", announced the commercial! I thought about it for an instant, and something in me just wanted to see if I could do it.

I didn't tell anyone I was going. I simply woke up, drove to the city, and waited in line to try out. I was a cheerleader in high school (big surprise, I'm sure), so I kind of knew what to expect regarding the process. I had never tried out for anything more official than high school teams (other than a stint at Six Flags Great America to dance and sing in their summer theater productions – which I **did not** make). Looking back, as I was always trying to figure out just where I belonged, performing was definitely something I enjoyed. I had dreams of working on a cruise ship and being a flight attendant, but neither of those ideas went further than researching (not because I didn't think it was possible).

Once I arrived at the tryouts, everyone was assigned a number (mine was 168). And then we waited to be called. I can still see the number pinned to my shirt. The selection team showed us a few moves to emulate, and we danced for the judges. For those of you Chicago natives, Andy Avalos, the NBC news weatherman, was one of the judges. He appeared regularly as a judge for these annual tryouts.

As is always the case with these events, there were several rounds of cuts. I kept making it past each round, until I was ultimately one of 16 remaining contestants. There were over 200 girls that tried out for the team. Now, I was in the top 16. I wasn't even thinking about the odds or any of that. I just did my best, danced as I loved to, and I kept advancing. I was so excited when I thought about the possibility of actually making the team! If instead, I had thought about the 8% chance that I would be in the final round of contestants, I probably wouldn't have focused on the possibility. This is why you shouldn't look at the odds first! Who says you won't be in the elite group?

That Saturday was a whirlwind. This was before cell phones and social media. No one could post about this (hence the announcement on the radio). Nobody knew I was there (except maybe my roommate, Jodie). And now I was in the final stages of being a "Luvabull" for the Chicago Bulls! At the end of tryouts, they informed us that the final 16 girls had to practice for several more days so the judges could get a better idea of our talents. We met at the McCormick Place conference center in a huge room and danced and practiced until the final roster was announced.

Ultimately, I didn't make it, but it was a thrill, nonetheless. It was a rush just getting that far, and it was exhilarating to think that I simply made a decision, showed up, did the work, and ALMOST made it. No fanfare, no hype, no sea of support. This was a huge confidence booster! It was so fun to tell everyone about my experience and how far I made it. I never thought once about not making it. I thought, if it's possible for someone, why not me? If they're having tryouts, why not give it a shot? I knew if I didn't go, I'd regret it. I had no idea what the chances were or how many people were going to show up.

Sometimes I think this is so much better, this "old" way of doing things: Not being able to research everything, no website to peruse, not knowing every little thing to expect, etc. Just having faith and going for it has a special attraction. I'm so glad I was thinking about the possibilities instead of the contrary. This has been the approach I've used for many turning points in my life. I have an idea, I ask about it, and then I try it. Why not me? Why not this?

Research is good. Research is necessary. Research just might not be full of possibilities, though, depending on what YOU want to see. So, when you're trying to do something new, or figure your way out of a problem, while positive thinking is indeed important, taking it a step further is vital, because in order to be happy, or feel joyful, you must view life as more than a struggle. Thinking you are a victim of your problem and that you can't do anything about it will not solve your problem; this will almost guarantee it won't be solved. But thinking about it as an opportunity to learn, to grow, to help someone else - this will change your perspective and your focus, and will shift your energy. Like the great Albert Einstein said, "You cannot solve a problem with the same mind that created it."

> "You cannot solve a problem with the same mind that created it."

If you're not in that negative mindset, you are going to create solutions much more quickly. *Pathways to Possibility*, by Rosamond Stone Zander, is a great book about addressing this negative thinking. In it, she talks about just how much negative thinking can impact us. Getting stuck in negative thinking makes us focus on survival. If we start to think about survival and all the things we don't have, trying to make the best of it, thinking about the risks (needing the right education, making the right connections, stressing about the competition), we find ourselves in a downward spiral, and we become more attached to what we're not getting, or what we don't have. And then we don't focus on the possibilities. Then ultimately, we don't try.

By reframing this perspective, no longer thinking about what you don't have and choosing instead to start adapting to the way things are (not the way you want them to be, etc.), you will begin to notice a shift in your energy. You can start thinking about who you **are** connected to, what you **do** have **now** to work with, what skills and talents are innate to you. Then the world begins to reflect this change. Suddenly (or what feels like suddenly), doors begin to open, and paths like joy, love, and gratitude are revealed, just radiating possibility! You start to notice that opportunities are coming your way. People are sending you messages to connect, articles are just appearing in your inbox, you're bumping into people that can help you. All of a sudden, someone that you haven't talked to in a while calls you and tells you about an opportunity that can help you.

This is all because you are radiating this possibility, and you are seeing things and situations in a clearer, more positive light. And guess what? People are attracted to that, and to you! This is no accident. You are getting these new opportunities because your mindset has changed, and your focus is different. It's like thinking you'll get in the longest line at the store, and then you see the other lines you are not in, evaporate. Just like you thought, right? But as soon as you think about it differently, your line shrinks! Let me share a story about this very concept.

I was in London on a business trip several years ago. I am the type of person that, although I like to plan and know what to expect, when I travel, I like to be surprised when I get there. I like to ask around, see where I am, feel the energy and what I'm drawn to, and then plan where I'll go. Arriving in a new place that is filled with possibilities is very appealing to me. Taking it all in when I get there, and seeing what's possible, is one of the many reasons I like to travel.

> Arriving in a new place that is filled with possibilities is very appealing to me.

I arrived in London, checked into my hotel, and promptly took a long-needed nap. (Although many of my friends will attest to the fact that I can fall asleep almost anywhere, I cannot stay asleep on planes.) Unfortunately, this means that when I arrive somewhere, I'm rarely rested and ready to go. This does not make for a very "possibility-filled" scenario. So, I don't resist it. I sleep so that I can have a better (filled with more possibilities) experience later.

After my nap, I grabbed a quick snack and started roaming around the city. This is one of my favorite things to do. I never know what I'll see, what the people will be like, what restaurants are nearby, etc. And that's the fun of it! Almost immediately, I saw one of those kiosks geared toward tourists, selling all kinds of tickets to local events. *The Lion King* was in London at that time and was all the rage. The show was selling out in cities all over the world. In Chicago, where I lived, shows were sold out for months. Although I wanted to go, I didn't investigate the possibility, chalking it up to, "Well, it's sold out; what am I supposed to do?" I probably don't have to tell you that this is exactly the type of negative mindset that will get you precisely **nothing**.

As I strolled around London, and dreamt, and thought about the possibilities for what I could or would do, I wandered over to the kiosk and asked about tickets to *The Lion King*. Of course, tickets were all sold out for the week I would be there. OK, I thought. Then I am meant to be doing something else that week. What else is possible? So off I went to explore other opportunities. At this point I didn't have my heart set on going. I was just open to letting the experiences unfold that I was meant to have.

The next morning, I was at the clients' office, and they were asking me about my plans for the week. "Let us tell you about some great places," they offered. I asked them about the shows. I told them I wanted to see *The Lion King*, but that it was sold out. "Oh, that's okay. We have this system here in London. You can go down to the theater at show time, and line up outside to see if any tickets become available. If there are any no-shows, extra tickets, etc., the theater employees will come outside and let you know. They sell them to you at face value, no less." This sounded too good to be true, because in Chicago, we have something similar, but these folks are not employees of the theater or the ballpark. These are folks who stand outside of the venue, trying to sell tickets back to you at a higher price, striving to make the most money possible from people who probably didn't plan accordingly.

I need to pause here and tell you that I was on this trip with a few of my colleagues - two women, to be precise. They probably wouldn't admit it, but I got the feeling they didn't like me very much. Not only that, but after hearing these clients tell me about how I just might be able to have what I wanted, these two women were not supportive of the idea. They told me very explicitly that I would never get in to see a sold-out show. I'm pretty sure they had plans to go see another show but didn't invite me to go along. I wanted to add this tidbit because they were not helping me with my "possibilities" mindset. I knew that listening to them would not get me what I wanted.

I preferred to listen to the people who were telling me that I just might be able to make it happen. Yes, these were my people! Isn't it funny when you come across perfect strangers who seem to want better things for you than people who know you? Actually, sad is a better way to say it; it's sad, not funny. At least those people are out there, though! Amen to that! (And please keep looking for these people!)

My workday ended and I left the office wondering about just **what might be** possible. I left the office annoyed that my coworkers didn't have any faith. I left the office feeling like a girl in junior high school who didn't get invited to the party. But I only felt like that for a few minutes. I knew wallowing in self-pity wouldn't make me feel better. And it certainly wouldn't help me to see *The Lion King*. So off I went. Off I went to see what exactly might just be possible.

Arriving at the West End theater district in London was surreal. As I mentioned before, I don't research much before traveling to new cities, so I didn't know what to expect. And this was only five years into the world wide web (the Internet, for you younger kids). But because I had to look up how to get there, I began to realize that this was a famous place. Famous like Broadway in New York. The taxi driver delivered me to the theater, where a long line of people filled the street. This is the line I was going to stand in. It was long. It was filled with

> It was filled with people who saw the possibilities.

people who saw the possibilities. People who hoped that they would get lucky. People who had faith. People like me.

So, I jumped out of the cab and promptly went to the back of the line. There had to be 50 people in front of me! Well, I'm already here, I thought to myself. I might as well stand in line for a bit. Who knows? Maybe there are 50 no-show seats just waiting to be filled. As I waited, just like my clients had explained, employees from the theater were coming out with tickets in their hands, looking to sell them at face value.

And then it happened. An employee was announcing that he had a ticket, **one** ticket. "Is there anyone in line who is by themselves? Who needs a single ticket?" Hmm, I thought. That's me! But of course, among the 50 people in front of me, there must be a few other "singles" who will certainly claim that ticket. But there weren't. There were groups of three and four, and couples hoping they'd get lucky. But not one person in front of me was a "single." **NOT ONE SINGLE PERSON**!

I waited patiently for someone to claim the ticket, getting a little excited but not feeling lucky. Then it was my turn. It happened. That employee came up to me and showed me the ticket (just like my clients said they would). He asked if I wanted to buy it. I was expecting it to be at least double the price (not believing they would sell these highly coveted seats at face value). I looked at the ticket and it said 20. That's 20 quid (quid=bucks for you US folks). I would have paid $100 to see this show. I was expecting to pay $100 to see this show. But there it was. A ticket to *The Lion King*, for 20 quid. "Yes, I'll take it!" I exclaimed. "Then come with me, please," the friendly theater worker replied.

Off to my seat, which of course I was expecting to be a mere undesirable seat. A seat stuffed in the back, with an obstructed view. I had no idea where I would be sitting, because I didn't know this theater, or this city for that matter. But either way, I thought… I will be seeing and hearing the most magnificent show in London, of all places!

As he guided me to my seat, we kept going toward the front, along some secret path that didn't look appealing. It felt like we were walking along some back aisle where no regular person would walk. I was wondering where he was taking me, but didn't want to seem too anxious, and I was grateful, obviously, so I just kept quiet.

We finally stopped behind a curtain and he opened the curtain to reveal four lovely seats inside a private viewing area. You know those seats in the balcony that you see in operas where the rich and famous people sit? Those expensive seats where you assume you must know the right people in order to be sitting there? (These seats are actually called "The Gods"; who knew?) Well, these were those seats. And no one was in them! I asked the guide if indeed he showed me to the right seat. He was sure he had. I thought it must be a mistake. He left, and I sat down sheepishly.

I couldn't believe my luck! I slowly took it all in. I was just waiting for him to come back and tell me that there had been a mistake. I waited and waited, certain he would reappear after he realized his blunder. But he never came back. Finally, one man walked in. He was in his mid-twenties, and unlike me, confident that he had the right seat. He said hello and told me he was glad at least someone was going to enjoy the show. What? I asked him why no one else was here. He said one person couldn't come, and that the other two seats belonged to his friends that were still at the pub and not interested in coming after all. Wow, this was unbelievable!

Here I was, watching the most popular show in London and beyond, in a seat fit for a queen, with an amazing view, and a nice, polite gentleman, who didn't try to hit on me (I had mentioned I was married). He was a good sport and even offered to show me where the refreshments were during the intermission. It was exhilarating, easy, enjoyable, and most of all, unforgettable. I just couldn't believe my luck. It was lucky. **I was lucky**.

But here's the thing. I never would have been there if I didn't think it was possible. If I hadn't shared my desire with the clients that day. If I had believed my coworkers who said I would never get into the show. If I had simply gone to dinner that night

> And because I did choose possibility, I was able to have this unbelievably surreal experience and a memory I will never forget!

instead of trying to see the show and get a last-minute ticket. Or even if I just walked by the kiosk, saw the show was sold out, and then never thought about it again. Believing all of those things, or doing anything differently, I never would have seen what was possible, and because I did choose possibility, I was able to have this unbelievably surreal experience and a memory I will never forget! (And a story I'm writing about in my first book.)

For those of you who are parents, or those in leadership roles, or those who manage people, or anyone who is part of a team, let's think about this as it applies to our personal and professional worlds: are you promoting this mindset or perspective at home and work? Are you promoting this with your team or kids? Are you, **AND** is your team, generous, responsible, flexible, and encouraging others to remain open to possibilities?

Having this perspective and embracing this mindset will give the people around you the opportunity to thrive at home and at work. You have this power, no matter where you are in the hierarchy. Really, you do have the power. It might not seem like that if you're not a manager, or if you don't have the promotion you want yet. But you always have a choice about your mindset. It's one of the only things you can actually control in your life. So, why not use this power for good?

Imagination is another way to cultivate this possibility mindset. Some of my research comes from a great book about how imagination leads you to what is possible. In the book, *Imagination First: Unlocking the Possibility* by Eric Liu and Scott Noppe-Brandon, the authors share their ideas about imagination, but they actually mention the *Art of Possibility* in their book, so their concepts come from that train of thought as well. It certainly does take some imagination to think about what's possible. This book discusses what it would be like if you could imagine something and couldn't do it, **versus** if you could imagine something and were able to look beyond your imagination and create it.

While we're talking about shifting perspective and thinking about positive thinking and opening your teams to a new way to frame what you're doing, think about this story from their book. This is a story about a young girl who is dreaming about becoming an astronaut. This young girl is contemplating her dream and she walks outside, looks up at the sky, and thinks about all these cool things and how big the universe is. She's outside thinking about how we are all connected and about what it would be like to be an astronaut and be able to see the world from another viewpoint: literally from a different view (in space). She gets so excited about what this would feel like, and how it could happen, (visualization is SO key, you guys), and she races to the house to tell her father about all of this. Running through the front door, the screen door slamming shut behind her loudly, she is out of breath with excitement. She runs up to her father and tells him her dreams, and you know what her father says? He retorts, "That's no life for a lady."

What? Really? Can you imagine this scene? Imagine being that little girl and hearing your father squash your dream. In one second, that little girl could go from really seeing the possibility, feeling what it would be like to be an astronaut and envisioning all of those awesome experiences, to thinking it will never happen, all with just a few words from her father. Maybe you don't have to imagine it. Maybe it happened to you. Maybe someone that raised you and loved you did this frequently. If that is the case, then I am so sorry. Just hearing this father's response makes my heart sink. This young girl isn't even thinking about how; she's just thinking about IF. And that's just it! Kids only think about and imagine the possibilities. These are the things kids are contemplating. While adults (the uninspired ones) are shutting them down, with little thought of how impressionable these young minds can be.

Most children at the age of 8 or so wouldn't even think to counter this statement or know how to tell their mom or dad they are incorrect. I'm guessing not many of you would have said to your own parents, "I don't care what you think. I'm going for it anyway." Not likely as a young child. It's not even that likely as a teenager, but certainly a little more likely. For some of you, this may just be motivation to prove the naysayers wrong. But for others, it's shutting the door to a possibility. It's crushing a dream. And it's so unnecessary. But even more so, it's particularly impactful to a young child.

I'm sure you can see now: imagination has to come first. At any age in life, we have these ideas; then, we begin to think about the possibility and how sweet it would feel to have or do or be that thing we imagine. And it's glorious! Can you feel it now? Can you remember how it felt when you wondered about possibilities as a kid? This period of life, when children are still young and impressionable, is so special, and requires supportive parents and adults around who can help guide those dreams, and help kids see just what imagination and creativity can bring to them, and to the world. Not many things have greater importance than this.

What if that little, eight-year-old girl, dreaming of going to outer space, was little Bonnie Dunbar? Bonnie is an engineer, a professor, a scientist, and a NASA astronaut. She is a veteran of five space flights. More importantly, Bonnie Dunbar had an idea, was open to the world of possibilities, and then went and pursued those possibilities. Maybe she had someone in her life that told her it wasn't possible, but I'm willing to bet she had someone showing her *how it was possible*. She put in the work, got the education and was able to make her dreams a reality. All because she knew it was possible!

> Imagination is that spark or idea in your head; without it, you're not going to be able to turn around and ask the right questions.

If Bonnie had a parent or a sibling that discouraged her and had said, "No, you can't do that," and kept her from her dreams, we wouldn't have an astronaut named Bonnie Dunbar, who was President of the Museum of Flight, led the University of Houston STEM Center, was a faculty member in the College of Engineering, and is a professor of aerospace engineering. She must be one fabulous lady (and someone I'd love to have on my podcast)! Without imagination and possibilities, we wouldn't have this astronaut who was able to make discoveries and share all this technology and engineering and leadership and science with our world, right? We wouldn't have her! You must be able to imagine it, right?

Imagination is that spark or idea in your head; without it, you're not going to be able to turn around and ask the right questions. If someone comes to you with a problem or an issue, you think about the problem and use your creativity to come up with ideas on how you may solve that problem. Then you sit down and brainstorm, collaborate, and see what will work best. Thus, imagination leads to creativity, and then innovation. In *Imagination First*, they say "the reality is that imagination comes first. It must." That spark, that idea, that concept comes first. It just does. You wouldn't go out and have the will to do something unless you had an idea to do it, right? "**Until and unless** we have the emotional and intellectual capacity to conceive of what does not yet exist, there is nothing toward which we can direct our will and our resources." (*Imagination First*)

We're trained from our earliest childhood to just believe what others are telling us—our parents, our guardians, our teachers, our bosses. But what if, instead, they said, "That's a great idea, why don't you think about that a little bit more; why don't you go explore that?" We're trained not to do that, yet it's so important.

So, first there's imagination, then there's creativity. That creativity is your imagination applied.

"The good news is, imagination is a muscle." In *Imagination First*, the authors discuss what you need to do to increase your potential for innovation, and that it is just like a muscle. The good news is, it can be toned and straightened and tightened just like the muscles in your body, right? "The bad news is, imagination is a muscle. Neglecting it leads to atrophy and enervation." Just like when you don't work out for a while, you're not exercising your body, and you begin to start losing your strength; you have to keep exercising and building muscle consistently. It's not something you can do once a month and then notice a difference.

Imagination works the same way. You have to tone that muscle. It requires daily exercise, and you have to give it attention so it can grow. Encouraging a strong and healthy imagination is just like working out. You have to continue to stay fit. You can't elevate your abilities without continuous practice. Just like with your physical fitness, you can't just say, "I really want to be fit," then not do anything for five days, then go outside and say, "I'm fit now." That's just not how it works.

Still, no matter how much we exercise our imagination, we might not always accomplish what we imagine. But we will certainly never accomplish what we refuse to imagine. This is in line with a well-known quote from Wayne Gretzky, a famous hockey player from Canada. He said, "You miss 100% of the shots you never take." Simply, you can't make a shot unless you take it. We're always telling our kids that, too. They love basketball and they often used to say things like, "I didn't know if I would make it." Well, you're certainly **not** going to make it if you don't even try to put the basketball in the hoop. It's the same thing with imagination. We're never going to accomplish what we refuse to imagine. So, let's start thinking about it and how it **CAN** happen, instead of how it won't.

> We're never going to accomplish what we refuse to imagine.

They say in *The Art of Possibility*, "In the universe of possibility you set the context and let life unfold. It's all invented anyway so might as well invent a story or framework of meaning that enhances our quality of life and the life of those around us." If you are going to imagine something, why not imagine it positively? If you're creating it in your mind, why not make it something positive, right? If you begin with that framework, it's going to enhance your quality of life. When you imagine something negative, it never makes you feel any better, right? Do negative thoughts help you come up with solutions or do they perpetuate even more negative things?

Have you ever seen that exercise about connecting the 9 dots in a square?

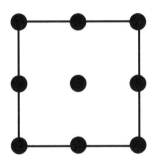

The premise is to instruct the student to try to connect every single dot using only four lines, without ever taking their pencil off the paper. Basically, the result people come up with is this drawing above and they look at it and think, "Well, I don't know if this is possible; I don't know whether I can do it without lifting my pencil from the paper." But the *only* instruction is that your pen cannot leave the paper. The instructions don't mention anything about staying in the lines, what shape to create, or how long the lines have to be. If you are a "think inside the box" type of person, you will rack your brain trying to figure out how it can be done. It will make you crazy!

But if you are the type of person that thinks outside the box, **about the possibilities that exist**, then you will be able to solve this puzzle rather easily. If you don't just consider that these four lines will make a box that you're used to seeing, you can solve the puzzle. When you consider this another way, without preconceived ideas or limitations, then when you're given the instructions, rather than focusing on what they didn't tell you (stay inside the lines, draw a box), then you become open to more possibilities.

The instructions just say, "Can you do this?" And our trained, narrow mind, tells us we have to stay inside the lines. Most people do not come up with the solution. But if you quite literally think outside of the box, and imagine something different, and think about what is possible, you will be able to solve this problem, and get this result. Your possibility-style thinking will solve this riddle, as seen below.

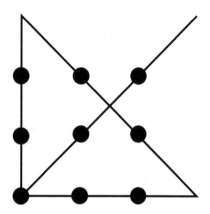

I wish I would have been ahead of the game when I was younger, but I, too, could not figure out how to connect the nine dots with just four lines. But, with a little extra imagination, this is what you can come up with. Why not do it, why not think outside the box? Why not reframe that possibility?

One of the concepts in *The Art of Possibility* is called "Lighting a Spark." This is encouraging the art and practice of generating a spark of possibility for others to share. What could be more beautiful than asking what's possible? Do you have passion, rather than fear? Do you have abundance, rather than scarcity? What are you bringing to the table? What are you putting out there in the universe? What are you

_____

What could be more beautiful than asking what's possible?

_____

imagining for yourself? When you open yourself up to possibility or you give yourself as a possibility to others, then you're ready to catch their spark. You're saying, "Here's what I'm offering you," and they can reply back to you, and then you're feeding off that energy, lighting sparks with each other.

"The life force for humankind is, perhaps, nothing more or less than the passionate energy to connect, express and communicate. *Enrollment* is that life force at work, lighting sparks from person to person, scattering light in all directions. Sometimes the sparks ignite a blaze and sometimes they pass quietly, magically, almost imperceptibly from one to another to another." (*The Art of Possibility*). This is a beautiful quote. Please stop and reread that, focusing on it for a moment.

I'm sure everyone has experienced this at one time or another. Sometimes you feel these sparks, don't you? Sparks with people, sparks with things, with energy and with excitement. Sometimes it's really subtle and magical, and you just get a feeling, and you go along your way. You say to yourself, "That was nice." Or maybe you complimented someone, and felt that energy from them after (or from you to them). You are the framework for everything that happens in your life. You always have an opportunity to light a spark.

I hope you're wondering by now, how do I/you create a framework for possibility? *The Art of Possibility* reminds us, "Purpose, commitment and vision are distinctions that radiate possibility." Being purposeful, committing to something, and having a vision all contribute to more possibilities. It's a desire in which any human being can resonate. It's showing someone that vision and having them say, "Yeah, yeah, I get what you're saying." It's that instant when any human being on that call or in that room can hear what you're saying and it's resonating with them. It's an open invitation with inspiration for people to create ideas. And the more we do that in our daily lives, in our work, with our families, the better we are and the more possibility there is out there on our planet!

In summary, I think of possibilities like this: Every experience we have, every person we meet, good or bad, is mirroring *something* inside of us. Think about that when you're interacting with people anywhere, anytime. Think about being creative and about what's possible, and then ask yourself, "What else is possible? If I can create this, what else could I do?" I encourage you to go find the more beautiful possibilities in all that you do. Reach out and help people to create that imagination and see what else is possible and do those things for each other that are lighting sparks and generating all kinds of positive experiences. Imagine if you didn't? We'd just have more of the same (and we already have plenty of that.)

Just in case you need one more story for encouragement, here is one from 3B.

I'm going to close this chapter with one of the most powerful experiences of possibility I had, when I decided to treat myself and upgrade my seat from economy to an exit row on a recent business trip back home to Chicago. Let me preface this by saying that I have only sat in a first-class seat one time in my life. I was working for America West Airlines (yes, back in 1998). I was flying standby, as employees are allowed to do, and I was lucky enough to score a seat in first class, after everyone had boarded. I felt guilty being up there in first class. (I have since learned that a person should only feel guilty if they have done something immoral, illegal, or unethical. Feeling bad doesn't equate to guilt. It shouldn't, anyway.)

Why did I feel bad? Because I was up there getting waited on, sipping champagne, eating delicious food, while a baby cried in economy class. I felt for that mom (I had a young child at the time). I just wanted to go back there and give her my seat so that she and the baby could have more room and be more comfortable.

I thought, "Who am I to be sitting in this seat?" I'm not sure if you've ever felt that way, but that was my struggle.

Back to this flight. On my first leg of this particular business trip, I was lucky enough to have an entire row to myself, and it was divine! Of course, it was! Who wouldn't love having all that space with no one coughing around you, etc.? On my return, when I checked in for my flight back to Chicago, there were a few exit row seats available for purchase. I think it was about $100 to upgrade to one of these seats. It took me a few minutes to spend the extra cash, but I told myself that the extra money, even if not covered as a business expense, was worth it so I could be more comfortable and experience a more peaceful, relaxed flight. I was willing to spend it. (But of course, the guilt crept back in.)

When I arrived at my newly purchased exit row seat, there was a man sitting in it. I was immediately annoyed, but still polite (we can always choose to be polite). He smiled and looked up at me and asked if I wouldn't mind changing my seat. In the back of my head I'm thinking, "Sir, I just paid $100 extra for this seat, I already feel guilty, and now I'm going to have to justify it, tell you no, or give it up?" Ugh! This was killing me! I was already second guessing my decision. As he sweetly explained, he wanted to sit next to his wife, who was seated in the middle exit row, and who couldn't change seats. Yeah, yeah, I thought. But this is what my husband/I would have done as well. This man wondered, would I be willing to switch seats with him? Again, how could I say no? As he asked me the question, he showed me his boarding pass, which was already displayed on his phone. **His seat was in first class!!!**

Yes, that's right. First class. He showed me the ticket on his phone and wanted to give me his first-class seat so he could sit next to his lovely wife in the exit row, in coach. How's that for possibility!?! So there I was, on my way home from SFO, in a first-class seat, enjoying all of the wonderful things that come with first class: a welcoming smile from the flight attendant, a warm hand cloth, a choice of beverages, and a snack etc. And the promise of more to come. And this was all because I wanted to treat myself to the possibility of a better seat.

Oh, and I forgot to mention that I was also debating when to board the plane. I hate to sit there on the plane and wait 30 minutes while everyone boards. Sometimes I get on when my group is called, and sometimes I wait. This time I waited. I'm not sure I would have had the same experience if I hadn't waited. If that man and his wife weren't already in those seats, it may have turned out differently. That was the universe guiding me again.

And so it goes with possibility. I imagined what it would be like to have a great seat. I had actually sent a text about wanting to experience a first-class seat to my friends on a different flight just a few months before. I took action and used my will to create it by buying the ticket to the better seat. And then I let the universe do the rest. Putting it into action is what it's all about. The possibilities are endless, but you have to take those steps. You have to commit to something, to take the risk, to be willing to have a regret or make a mistake. I never would have been traveling home via first-class if I hadn't chosen to buy the exit row upgrade. I'm so glad I did. Thank you, Mr. Jones!

> You have to commit to something, to take the risk, to be willing to have a regret or make a mistake.

Possibility is the secret that exhilarates you and keeps you feeling enthusiastic about life. When you look at every situation or opportunity, starting each day thinking about what is possible, you will feel bigger, lighter, more abundant, and more positive. The world needs this so desperately, so we can create a planet with lots of sparks. Ready? Go!

2

. . . . .

Connection

(That's the answer and I didn't
even know it was the question)

Human beings are social creatures. Even the introverts
among us have an innate need for human interaction.
Whether we consider ourselves an introvert or an
extrovert, we all have one thing in common: we feel the impact
of not being able to interact with people. We long to be connected.
We require connection.

About four years ago, I attended a leadership conference, and
for two days I was trying to articulate my vision as the facilitator
had encouraged us. Her main goal was to help us figure out:
what's your mission? I didn't have one. But to my surprise, on the
last day, in the last 15 minutes actually, I had an idea! And it just
so happened that the one person in the room—one of only five
men out of 150 attendees—was present and available to connect
to! This is how I began the next phase of my career developing
people, which resulted in speaking to almost 3000 people over
the next eight months!

This unbelievable moment of connecting started with me
racking my brain for two days, trying to figure out what I wanted

to build, what was missing from my work, what was the next thing I could focus on to take my life from "pretty good" to awesome. Attendees at this conference were encouraged to cultivate a special program or mission that we were passionate about. While I participated in the breakout sessions, listened to others' stories, and completed the exercises as instructed, I wasn't finding that "thing."

I'm pragmatic. Even if I didn't get that big idea, I realized that if I learned one or two new things, it would be worth my time. I live for those moments that make you say to yourself, "Hmm, I hadn't thought of that." While I wasn't planning on having any life-changing moments, I would have been happy just meeting new people, hearing some inspiring stories, and then leaving with a few new words of wisdom. But that's not what happened.

At the conference, the final exercise instructed us to take 15 minutes and interact with as many people as possible, find out what they were trying to achieve, see if you had any tips/ideas for them, and then swap roles and share your story/idea. Then repeat the whole process with another person. The whole point of this exercise was to show us how helpful it can be to get someone else's perspective, and subsequently, their idea/question would prompt you to have new insight. Rapid connections! I thought this was brilliant! Such a simple, impactful exercise. I highly recommend trying this the next time you have the opportunity.

On this day, in the last few moments of the conference, I still did not have an idea to share. Or so I thought. So, instead of looking for someone to help me, I went straight to the person for whom I had an idea. I so desperately wanted to connect with this speaker from the conference. His story touched me deeply, and I wanted him to continue sharing it with as many people as possible. I had two teenage boys at the time, and I kept thinking about how kids their age could benefit from hearing this particular speaker's experiences.

So, I made a bee-line to him. When we introduced ourselves, he asked me right away, 'What do you need help with?' I excitedly told him that I didn't need help with anything, but that I wanted to help him. I quickly explained that I was so moved by his story that it brought me to tears. I told him that he should be speaking at colleges and high schools all over the country, and that I wanted to help him connect with people. He thanked me and then asked again what I wanted support with. Then, just in that one moment, I had a clear vision of what I wanted to create. And I told him: "I want to help people at my company feel more con-nected because I am feeling very disconnected" (a solution to a problem). He said that I should

> "I want to help people at my company feel more connected because I am feeling very disconnected"

go talk to one of the leaders at my company, who just happened to be at the conference. He pointed to him and said, "Go get in line."

I told him that I couldn't possibly take up my colleague's time when there were so many people waiting to speak to him. I didn't think it would be fair to all of the others who wouldn't have access to him after that day at the conference. I explained that I could talk to this leader when I got back to work, via email...someday. And he said, "You're going to do it now." I thanked him and shook my head no.

But he wouldn't settle for that. He told me, in no uncertain terms, that he was going to watch me as I waited in line to be sure that, indeed, I did speak to this leader. He actually grabbed my hand and dragged me across the room - gently, of course - toward the leader. There I was, waiting in line, listening to the other stories and ideas, and thinking I wasn't worthy to be in this position.

As I inched closer to the front of the line, I was completely blank as to what I wanted to say. I thought about starting off with,

"You know what the problem with our company is…" How many people would be excited to have a conversation with a person who started it with those words? Not many, as you can imagine. This is exactly what you **never want to say** to someone you're about to ask for help. (See many, many business books about this very topic.)

I knew in that moment, before it was just about my turn, that I SHOULD NOT open with that question. I knew, through many years of climbing the corporate ladder, that leaders want solutions, not problems. If you come to them with a problem, you better have at least one idea on how to solve that problem. Alternatively, if you came to them with a problem, you would likely be assigned the task of solving that problem. The same works for parents and kids. No Bueno!

I reached the front of the line, and finally it was my turn. I paused, took a deep breath, and introduced myself. "Hi there. My name is Julie and I work for our company." And then, all of a sudden, I had the exact words I needed. (This is the power of showing up even if you don't have all the answers.) I began with, "Do you think (our company) could benefit if everyone felt more connected?" And he smiled, and said "Yes, yes, yes!" I'm not kidding! He said yes **three times**!

> This is the power of showing up even if you don't have all the answers.

What? Am I in the twilight zone? Did I hear that right? Am I really talking to this senior leader in my company right now, and did he just say "yes" to my idea? **What is my idea anyway?** And then it just started pouring out of me. "I think it would be great if we could offer a way to connect people, regularly, in this virtual world we work in, so that people around the world could know we all share things in common. I will pick a universal topic and ask people to tell their stories. " He smiled again at me, and said,

"**And I will help you**. I will ask people to speak at these webinars, and I will even volunteer to speak at your first session." What???

What just happened? I presented an idea (that came out of nowhere), I have the support of leadership (from someone I've never met), and now I have support to help get others on board? As I looked over at my new friend (the one that literally pulled me to this line), he was smiling from ear to ear. So, of course, I ran over and I told him what just happened, and now I'm beaming from ear to ear. I was bursting with excitement and electricity! And he is not at all surprised.

The moral of this story: have the guts in the moment to step out of your comfort zone and be courageous. You never know what kind of connection you'll make. If I hadn't wanted to help the speaker that touched me so deeply at this conference, I would have never had the conversation about the problem that I wanted to solve. And I would have never started on my path to delivering the exact kind of training that I had been longing to deliver. In the end, my problem was feeling disconnected. My solution was to help others feel more connected. I connected to that speaker, and he connected me to that leader. Connections people!

Fast forward a few months to my downtown office (which I rarely visited because my team was in all different cities). I am walking down the hall, and I literally bump into the senior leader (neither he nor I are ever in this office), and I gently remind him that he said he'd support my initiative and tell a story at my workshop. I told him the topic would be based on a book I was reading. He told me to send him a link to the book and schedule the day on his calendar. My first workshop was delivered in January.

The result: over 300 people from all over the world joined the webinar. A few senior leaders shared stories, and folks were buzzing on the chat feature about how cool it was to hear these personal stories and make connections with these folks. No one could believe how many people were on the call and we were all amazed at the great turnout. I guess I was right: people wanted to feel more connected. I was craving that, and so were they! Hallelujah! Now, for next month! Was it a fluke? I certainly hoped not.

> I guess I was right: people wanted to feel more connected.

That week after, the emails kept coming. Emails with questions. What's up with this session you just delivered? How'd you make it happen? How'd you get so many people to attend? How did you get the stories? Well, I explained, I just asked. I had a solution to something I thought was a problem and followed through on it. I planned, I researched, I scheduled, I learned how to execute, and I delivered. In summary, I did the work. With my idea and hard work, I pulled it off. **And then I wanted to do it again.**

How did I pick the next topic? I let the universe guide me. Instead of pounding the pavement and racking my brain, I just waited to see what topics came up. I waited to see which emails I received, which articles I was reading, or what books I'd see recommended. A book would land in my lap or an article would appear in my email, and I'd have my next topic. But I was nervous; what if the first webinar was a fluke? What if no one showed up to the second webinar?

I picked another topic, I planned, I researched, I created the content, and I sent the invitations. You never know exactly how many people are going to show up, because although they may accept the invitation, on the day of the session, things come up. As always, I just thought to myself, whoever shows up is exactly the right group of people to attend. Whoever shows up will be open to the message and will be happy to be there.

The date of the second session arrived, and I joined the call. And to my surprise and delight, it happened again. I watched as the numbers ticked up and up on the call, tallying higher each time someone new joined the call. Ten, twenty, thirty, fifty. Awesome, I thought! Fifty people have joined and that's at least 50 people I can connect and inspire today.

Then the numbers kept climbing, and finally we were past 300, just like the first time! WHAT???? Is this really happening? The funny thing about this number is that the maximum capacity on our conference call system was 250, and there shouldn't have even been 300 people permitted to join the call. But when I set up the call, there was a setting that didn't get saved and more people **could** actually join. So here we were again. **What was happening?** Connection, that's what. Let me explain more. Let's talk about the different types of connections.

What is so important about connections?
The Four Corners of Connection

"As long as you are alive, your heart and mind and soul will be searching for a connection. Another: several others. A community that will bring life, all the ingredients of life that you need to get past the limit of your present existence and performance. The need for connection begins before infancy and continues throughout life – from the womb to the tomb. If you are alive, you need it to thrive, period." I wanted to learn more about why connections were so important, and I stumbled upon a book (given to me by someone I just

> That day, when I made those connections, it was genuine.

happened to be mentoring) called *The Four Corners of Connections, The Power of the Other* by Doctor Henry Cloud. The quote above is from his book.

A great example of a good connection is the experience I had during the final exercise at the conference. That day, when I made those connections, it was genuine. When I approached the first speaker, I sincerely wanted to help him get his message out there. And the connection with that senior leader was because I thought, 'I can't be the only one feeling this way about connecting, and I am not going to hurt anyone by asking about my idea,' and that's why I did it.

Henry Cloud's book discusses four types of connections, and the better the connections, the more phenomenal and tremendous an impact they will have. Let's break them down.

The first type of connection is the corner-one connection, called *Disconnected*. The corner-one connection is summarized like this: there is either no connection or you feel disconnected to this person. This person is shallow, they're isolated, they don't provide feedback. They can't be vulnerable. You have increased stress around this person; you have low energy; you're not motivated; you procrastinate; you don't have clarity; you can't focus very well. You are not able to make a real emotional investment with this person and vice versa.

The second type of connection, corner two, is the *Bad Connection*. This is someone that you feel drawn to and that you feel a pull from (hopefully, this is a very small number). These are people you just keep trying to please, but you never quite get there. You just don't quite do what they need done. This might be a parent, a boss, a co-worker, or someone in your personal life.

With your corner two connections, no matter what you do it doesn't work, and you're not sure why, but you keep trying, and you keep running up against a wall. These people are withholding praise from you. They're critical and they have unreasonable demands. The result from connecting to a person like this in your life is bad performance. You end up being defensive; you have a diminished passion for whatever it is you're doing, personally or professionally. Obviously, this is a connection you want to try to avoid as well.

The corner-three connection is the *Pseudo-Good Connection*, which is all about feeling good. This connection is described as having an endorphin high around this person, but this is temporary. You're always striving to find one more good feeling. The problem is that, after the endorphin high, you go back to feeling low. You think that you liked that great feeling, and you want that back again. But when you get it, there is always the inevitable low that follows.

If you're focusing on a bad connection, a pseudo-good connection, or a connection with someone that you just cannot please, by just banging your head against a brick wall and trying to change it, you're not going to have any success. You want to get to the corner-four connection—this true connection—which is the best one! This is about being connected in a positive way, in an impactful way, and in a way that helps you grow.

The corner-four connection is a place where you can be your real authentic self. Authenticity means you're not changing anything about yourself to be in that relationship or that interaction. You are the same, no matter what situation you're in. I'm not talking about being polite when you'd like to tell someone off. This is common, grown-up courtesy.

The corner-four relationship builds ownership, responsibility, and autonomy. This type of connection allows you to admit, "I am responsible for my problems, my solutions, my life, and my choices. I take ownership of these things." The other person in this corner-four relationship makes sure you're doing that but gives you the independence to find the right path on your own, with support. This relationship makes learning and failure safe. You can learn lots, you can fail, and you will be just fine. You are going to be guided and supported, but you're going to be held accountable as well. This is a connection/a relationship to which you can bring your heart, mind, soul, and passion. You'll know when you're in a corner-four relationship because when you leave a conversation, you feel energized, having the courage and confidence to work out issues. (Incidentally, this is also important in parenting; see my next book.)

What is the impact of truly great connections— the corner-four connections? Doctor Cloud wrote, "These are the things that can happen if you have truly great connections in your life and the more great connections you have, the more of this you get." I'm sure you'll agree, the results are pretty spectacular.

#1: You live longer. Of course, you live longer! The research shows happily married people actually live longer; people that have happy relationships with friends, and even people with dogs, also live longer. People with more great connections have longer lives. Period.

#2: Great connections determine whether you reach your goals. They determine what your salary is. Also, believe it or not, your kids' academic success is impacted by *your* corner-four connections. Think about that for a minute: your truly great connections impact your children! It makes complete sense.

#3: Your connections determine how you cope with stress and failure. For some people, when something bad happens to them, the world just ends. We all know people like this. They find out some bad news, like maybe they need a new washing machine. And their entire day is ruined (i.e., "I can't believe this is happening to me again!") But when you have more corner-four connections, you don't see these incidents in the same light. It's not doomsday just because an

> When you have better connections in your life, you handle stress and failure more easily.

appliance broke down. When you have better connections, you are inspired more, and have the resources to help you cope. When you have better connections in your life, you handle stress and failure more easily.

#4: Your personal pain threshold is higher. Yes! You read that right! You can actually tolerate pain better when you have better connections in your life. Let that sink in for a minute. By having better connections in your life, your physical body can tolerate more pain than someone who has fewer good connections. If that isn't proof that our minds and bodies are connected, then I don't know what is!

#5: Great connections help determine, and impact, what you think. They affect us physically, emotionally, intellectually, and spiritually; and then they help us find our purpose in life. This is a really important point. When you are connected to truly great people, you get closer and closer to your purpose. You are going to get there, because you have people that are connected and interested in supporting you.

What else is good about these connections? Truly connected people are both emotionally present and able to give and receive. I'm sure you've experienced a great connection where you've had an engaging conversation back and forth. This can happen at work, at home, or with a random stranger at the grocery store. You're meshing with a person, and you're getting more energy when you talk to them. You hear yourself saying, "That's a great point" or "I totally agree." Everyone has been in conversations like this. Those are true connections.

They also come from many different dimensions of life, like a great coach or a phenomenal teacher. I've had some great teachers growing up. I've had great bosses, mentors, and colleagues. And then there are those great leaders that you don't even actually know, but that you feel connected or drawn to—people that you want to be around or people you want to read about or know more about. You want to be connected to them because they have all these traits that we have been talking about. They are affecting you positively and you want to be connected to them.

In the end, we all have the same fundamental human needs, and there are a lot of them, but the way to meet them is quite simple and straightforward. You have to have honest feedback; you have to have a connection; you have to have someone that supports you; you have to be honest; and you have to be real. All of these important ideals can only come from true connections. You can't control others, but you can control how you respond to things, by making more great connections so you can be healthier, and live in a world where you're supported, embracing who you truly are.

> All of these important ideals can only come from true connections.

Dr. Cloud also wrote about experiments that were part of his research for the book. One study concluded that babies who had less physical touch and connections actually had differently wired brains. Not having those early connections negatively impacted their behavior later in life, all because they didn't have the human connection they needed to thrive. So, if you don't think connections are important, the research and the science prove otherwise: You must feel connected to thrive.

Want to get there sooner? Then ask yourself: do you want to grow, and if you do, who else wants that for you? What are you being challenged to do in your life, personally or professionally, that someone is asking you to do more of than you're doing now? Those are the people that want to see you succeed, and they want you to thrive. The people that are chiming in and saying, "Here's how I think you can improve" are great connections. Whether professionally or personally, be open to that feedback and to those connections, because those are the people who are going to be supporting you to get to the next level. Who is giving you both support and input? Where and with whom can you be who you are and be free to explore?

I'm grateful to have many good friends, old and new, and an incredibly supportive spouse. I'm in my fifties now, and I have friends from high school, friends from ten years ago at work, and new friends I've met within the last few years. All of these friendships and relationships are corner- four connections. I built these intentionally. I encourage you to reach for these corner-four connections whenever and wherever you can. It's the best way to live!

Connection is the secret that started it all (for me, anyway). Every one of us on the planet longs for it. We all have the power to generate it. We can seek it out in every situation. As a result of connection, we leave each situation as a more filled-up person, a person who wants to keep it going. Connect, always. You will never regret it.

3

. . . . .

Mindfulness and Focus

(And not multitasking)

We hear about meditation and mindfulness a lot more these days than we used to. But why? It's because we're all so stressed and need help to relax and ease our tension. Daily, we're doing more than we've ever done. We work more hours, have more responsibilities, and seem to have less time. No wonder we're stressed out!

As we work remotely from our homes more often and work in front of technology all day, we're sitting more and moving less. Our worlds are consumed by technology, and it is pure overload. We have multiple streams of notifications coming at us from different devices. Even if we like our technology, having all of this coming at us at one time isn't good for our brains or our bodies. Our technology has enabled us to be available 24/7. But what is this doing to us?

Can we just put our phone in another room and eliminate all the issues? Yes and no. The reason why this doesn't work completely is because, while you can eliminate external distractions, this doesn't necessarily eliminate internal distractions. It's incredibly challenging for us to stay focused on one thing. Most people will tell you it's tough for them to focus. Luckily, there are things we can do to help – and that don't cost us anything!

This is where mindfulness comes in. In a classic definition offered by John Kabat-Zinn, a US physician and founder of mindfulness-based stress reduction, he describes mindfulness as: "Staying on purpose in the present moment without judgement." It's about being focused on right now and on whatever is right in front of you.

If we think about mindfulness as concentrating on one thing at a time, is it the opposite of multitasking? Doing one job? Performing one task? Focusing on one thing in the present moment? This could be on your computer, something you're writing, or someone you're talking to. Being present is being mindful. When you're taking it all in, you're being mindful. And when you're being mindful, your body and mind are SO much healthier. To top it off, when you're multitasking, you're only 40% effective at any of those tasks. Who wants to do anything at 40% effectiveness? Wouldn't it be better to be 100% effective at each thing you did?

> When you're multitasking, you're only 40% effective at any of those tasks.

While meditation is about observing your thoughts without making judgments about them, mindfulness involves actually thinking and processing, and engaging in contemplation of each moment in time as it occurs. The practice of meditating will get you to a more mindful state more easily. Mindfulness is the state of being mindful, conscious, or aware. Being mindful is being present in a moment and really just focusing on what someone is saying to you. Being mindful will be easier if you have a meditation practice.

The practice of meditating actually changes your brain chemistry (more on how later), and when that changes, the state of awareness/consciousness is easier to get to. When we're in the state of conscious awareness and are fully present in the moment, being non-judgmental comes easier because you're just focusing on what's happening then and there. But also, you're acknowledging your thoughts and emotions of that very moment. Each moment is unfolding as it's happening.

Let's just say you could do this. What would contentment or letting go look like? What if you were just enjoying being outside, in the rain? Or as you look at a body of water, feeling the sun hitting your face or the breeze through your hair would be very peaceful. Joy and calm can be yours in any moment, when you're being mindful and present, aware of all the beautiful things you're feeling or seeing. When we're practicing this, we are directing our attention to our experience, as it unfolds. This is being present. This is reflecting on how you're feeling (joyful, calm, content, serene).

What about when you're talking to someone? What would it be like to have a conversation with someone who was *really* present? Contrast that with a conversation you've had with someone who wasn't in the moment. It's not a good feeling when you're trying to express yourself and that person isn't listening. We've all experienced talking to someone who is distracted; they are looking away, they're on their phone, etc. They are just not engaged in the conversation. Their mind is somewhere else. They are not being mindful. These types of conversations aren't pleasant. I'd rather be by myself than across the table from someone who is distracted and not paying attention to what I'm saying and sharing.

> Being mindful, and ultimately present, allows you to be in a totally aware state of mind, where you are better at responding more skillfully, to good or bad situations.

Being mindful, and ultimately present, allows you to be in a totally aware state of mind, where you are better at responding more skillfully, to good or bad situations. When something good is happening, you'll have the right words to describe it. It is easier for you to respond and be more thoughtful because your brain now has more gray matter (I'll explain this more a little later), and it's stronger and more prepared for you to competently respond. You have more empathy and more compassion regarding the interaction and the person with whom you're communicating.

Because you are forming your thoughts more easily, and have more clarity and focus, you'll get to what you want to say more quickly, and your feelings and concerns for others will improve. All of those benefits are coming because you are focusing more clearly and processing your thoughts better. Your focus on that person is improved, and everything that comes from that interaction is enhanced.

According to *The Huffington Post*, we have approximately 50,000 to 70,000 thoughts per day. That's about 2,100 thoughts per hour and a whopping 35-48 thoughts PER MINUTE. No wonder we think we'll have a hard time meditating. Who wouldn't? Everyone has busyness in their lives. We all have a lot going on. I despise the phrase, "I'm so busy". It's often used as a badge of honor. But it's redundant, if you ask me. We're all busy! Say something original! Let's talk about something specific. OR, even better: let's do something about it so it's not the first thing you say every time you see someone, and they ask you how you're doing. Beginning a meditation practice **can** and **will** help break you of this habit. You'll still be busy, but you will have more clarity and space for answering this question less reactively.

Can you imagine a world where we say, "I'm awesome and I feel great", when someone asks how it's going? Every day of our lives, we have things to do, people to see, appointments to go to, errands to run, meetings to attend, calls to make, tasks to complete, and more. This won't ever go away! Our lives will always be filled with things to do, albeit some days will be fuller than others.

And if you're reading this in 2021, some months there will be even less to do because we've been forced to follow guidelines for our own health and the safety of others. This is one of the gifts of being forced to slow down. Then, some days, no matter how much we have to do, we won't feel up to doing any of it. This is our body's way of telling our brain that we're done for a little bit. We're made to rest. Another gift. Being mindful will help us determine what's best to do in the moment, each day.

Think about a snow globe for a minute. Once you shake it up, you see thousands of snowflakes falling. In relation to meditation, each of the snowflakes represents distractions and thoughts that we have in our minds. Some of us have a ton of snow flying around, and for some of us it may take a longer time for the snow to settle. Meditation takes those thoughts and distractions and helps us see those thoughts as floating by, and finally resting on the bottom of the fluffy white ground, settled and at peace. No matter how long it takes, the noise in the world finally calms down as your mind slows down. Just because we have lots of thoughts—it doesn't mean we can't get to a place of mindfulness, contemplation, and introspection.

> Just because we have lots of thoughts—it doesn't mean we can't get to a place of mindfulness, contemplation, and introspection.

If you're especially feeling overwhelmed, this is even more of a reason to practice meditation. You may be thinking, "I can't clear my head long enough to meditate." I wish I had a dollar for everytime I heard this objection. Mindfulness is not about pretending that you don't have other thoughts. It's about training your mind to make all those thoughts fall to the bottom of that snow globe. When you're meditating, you're acknowledging those thoughts and you're trying to stay calm while you do it. You're noticing them and letting them float away without judgement.

The purpose of meditation is to calm your mind **even though** you have a thousand thoughts.

Whether you're a man, a woman, young, old, work for someone else or yourself, have kids, no kids, ailing parents, etc., we all have a lot going on. But we always have a choice about what we're doing, how we're doing it, and what we are focusing on as we're doing it. You can acknowledge your thoughts, and not judge them. Getting to a place where you are focusing on one thought at a time is being present and experiencing that thought. And the result is simply less stress.

So, if you're thinking you might want to try this (and I so hope you do), I have some good news for you! Did you know that the daily practice of meditation, even just five minutes a day, can change your brain chemistry to offset all of these negative effects of stress? Really, it's true. It seems too simple to have that kind of impact, but the **practice** is that powerful.

How? When you *practice* meditation and are being more mindful on a regular basis, you are creating more gray matter in your brain. That gray matter produces some amazing effects on your emotions and reactions. What types of amazing effects am I talking about? Well, just to name a few:

- Your creativity increases
- Your compassion increases
- You have more self-awareness
- Your memory improves
- Your focus improves
- You feel calmer and more peaceful
- You have better insight
- You sleep better
- You actually feel less pain!

https://www.inc.com/jessica-stillman/how-meditation-rewires-your-brain-for-less-anxiety-and-faster-learning.html

https://blog.bufferapp.com/how-meditation-affects-your-brain

Again, as you meditate regularly, you create more gray matter in your brain, which promotes all of these wonderful effects. There is an abundance of scientific research documenting this concept. "Mindfulness practice decreases activity in the parts of the brain responsible for fight-or-flight and knee-jerk reactions while increasing activity in the part of the brain responsible for what's termed our *executive functioning*. This part of the brain, and the executive functioning skills it supports, is the control center for our thoughts, words, and actions. It's the center of logical thought and impulse control."

> Again, as you meditate regularly, you create more gray matter in your brain, which promotes all of these wonderful effects.

https://hbr.org/2017/01/spending-10-minutes-a-day-on-mindfulness-subtly-changes-the-way-you-react-to-everything

When people implement a regular mindfulness practice, they experience thickening in their prefrontal cortex. This is the front of the brain, just above your eyebrows, and the area of your brain that's responsible for things like organizing, planning, executive functions, decision making, etc. For you proud multi-taskers, it turns out, the brain itself is really not able to be in two places at once. Mindfulness (and more gray matter) trains your brain to think only about the present moment. And thankfully, and lucky for you, more happiness is found in the present moment.

Another part of the brain that is affected through meditation is the amygdala. The amygdala is like the fire alarm in your body. If something happens to upset you, the amygdala fires. It goes way back to the days when our ancestors were chased by sabretooth tigers. When they encountered a threat like this, they had to make a decision quickly—whether to fight or to flee, or whether they were going to just freeze. So, although our amygdala, unfortunately, still operates in that way, with a consistent mindfulness practice—and there is a ton of research to prove this—the reactivity of the amygdala can begin to diminish.

Can you imagine, for example, with your brain chemistry changed, being better able to respond appropriately when you get that nasty email from a colleague or that snide remark from a stranger? You won't be as tempted by that usual gut reaction to want to fire back some sort of response. Instead, with a consistent mindfulness practice and the strengthening of attention, you'll have a little bit of space to be able to manage your emotions better. You're able to stay focused on one thing, even though you see three or four other things swirling around. And consequently, you have fewer regrets, and are more adaptable. Doesn't this sound more appealing?

To help you start your regular practice, I'm going to recommend an app I stumbled upon when researching this topic. There are many apps to use that will benefit you and contribute to this life-changing practice. I use an app called Breethe, which costs just a few dollars a month. I've been using it for over three years now. When I started using it, I committed to using it for 30 days, so that I could report back on my research for a workshop. I wanted to have examples of how it made me feel and the impact it had on my day and my work. I thought I would just try it, report on it, and then get back to my regular routine. But something else happened.

When the 30 days were over, I didn't want to stop using it. Why? I felt better. I was calmer. My day was better. I had more focus and clarity on tasks I was working on. I was more positive. I felt more serene and patient with my kids. I felt more compassion for people. And in stressful situations, not only was I able to keep my mind calm, and not be so reactive, but it was easier for me to calm down afterward.

Another added bonus: I taught myself how to breathe when I was in stressful situations. If I was on a plane and it wasn't going as planned, waiting was easier. When faced with an unexpected delay, I would immediately put meditation into practice. I didn't need to have the app playing on my phone. I was able to implement those habits which had become automatic over those 30 days, and now I had a new tool.

They say it takes 21 days to make something a habit. Because I committed to doing it for 30 days, I formed a new habit. My mind and body were

> I was able to implement those habits which had become automatic over those 30 days, and now I had a new tool.

used to it, and I built it into my routine. It's funny how those new skills work. If we just commit to doing something, and follow through, it's amazing what type of results we can have.

One nice thing about this app is that it's not just music and sounds. Music is great if it works for you—please use whatever works for you. I need more guidance. Breethe offers many choices. Users can pick a topic that they'd like to focus on and meditate on that. For example, they have separated their topics into "Achieve Success", "Feel Happier", "Improve Relationships", and even "Dealing with Loneliness". Simply click on the topic you'd like to focus on, and you have several choices. You're guided through visualizations that concentrate on that topic. For those of you who have a harder time focusing at first and feel like you can't just let thoughts pass by, this is helpful. Your mind has something to focus on, and you concentrate on that topic and get clearer on what you want to feel. You're meditating and learning how to feel more "fill in the topic," simultaneously.

Finally, if you're still resisting these concepts, I encourage you to try your own experiment for 30 days. Commit to it and do it. No one thing "out there" is going to change your attitude/brain/experience in any given moment. Only you have the power to do that. You **can** do it with meditation. Your brain and body need this. If it seems selfish to devote this time to yourself, then remember something just as important: everyone around you will also benefit. Start with just 5 minutes a day and feel the astounding results. And remember this great quote from the Breethe newsletter:*"Worrying does not take away tomorrow's troubles. It takes away today's peace."* And peace is what we're going for!

> "Worrying does not take away tomorrow's troubles. It takes away today's peace."

Being mindful is the constant secret. You can do it in every moment, every day of your life. You just have to choose. Choose to look someone in the eye. Choose not to pick up your phone in the silence. Choose to ask the question. Choose to stay quiet and take it all in. Mindfulness is for your mind, heart, and soul. And for the person you are in the moment with. Honor and cherish that. Who knows if you'll ever get the chance again?

4

. . . . .

Curiosity

(It's really as simple as wondering)

Being curious is as simple as saying, "Tell me about you, or tell me about what you do, or tell me about where you're from," and is a great way to start a conversation or invite someone to share their story. People love sharing their stories! People love talking about themselves! They want to be asked about who they are, how they are, and what they think. There is no easier way than to just ask. Be curious! "Curiosity is such a basic component of our natures that we are nearly oblivious to its pervasiveness in our lives." *https://www.ncbi.nlm.nih.gov/pmc/articles/PMC4635443/*

I grew up always curious about the world around me. I was the one in class who constantly had my hand up to ask questions. I was always contemplating what the teacher was saying. As you may know, asking questions comes naturally for toddlers as they learn about the world and try to figure out their place in it. It's this simple curiosity that helps them grow. And as adults, it's no different. It is this simple curiosity that helps **us grow**.

> It is this simple curiosity that helps **us grow**.

In a recent poll I conducted for this topic, I asked how people perceived their own level of curiosity, and between 60 - 80 percent of people considered themselves curious. The world is an amazing place and staying curious keeps it that way. I'm sure you can think back to a time when you wondered more about the world around you. As we get older, this seems to lessen, but we always have those topics or hobbies that continue to spark curiosity. It's exactly these topics that we should continue to move toward—move toward for work, move toward to connect with people, and move toward for happiness. Because if we can, if we do, we will have such a sweeter existence on this planet (remember above: more enjoyment and fulfillment?)

And then also, sometimes, because of curiosity, our experience is just simply delightful! I was recently on vacation, waiting in a hotel lobby for the shuttle back to the airport. While I waited, a pleasant woman was handing out conference badges and welcoming folks. I had seen her earlier in the day and walked by the table a few times, trying to figure out what the conference was all about. Finally, I just wandered over, and out of curiosity, simply asked, "What's this conference all about?" And she graciously answered. As I talked with her and asked her where she was from, etc., she and I bonded over her move to the area, because my son had just moved there recently also. She gave me a little advice to share with him, and it suddenly occurred to me to ask whether the conference hired speakers.

She said, "Yes!" Yes, they held three conferences each year, and they hired speakers for all of them. I didn't even think about doing this until I was in that moment, **after** I was curious about what she was doing. Then, before I could even ask, she gave me her phone number and email address. I told her I would be in touch soon. Just from being curious about someone else, I had someone interested in my work and a prospective new client.

And, to top it all off, as I walked away, she called me back. She wanted to give me something. **She wanted to give ME something!** She had a really nice canvas bag full of snacks and goodies that she was handing out to the conference attendees, and she wanted me to have one because I had been so nice. I was simply being curious!

During the course of my research, I was incredibly surprised to read that the central ingredient to creating a **fulfilling life** is, indeed, curiosity! To learn that being fulfilled—which is definitely a product of being happy and feeling content in your life—starts with being curious; that was captivating! Webster's Dictionary defines curiosity as being inquisitive and interested, as the desire to learn or know more about something or someone; what we feel when we are struck with something novel.

After reading this, I remembered a time when my older son was little, and how people used to stop me and say, "He seems really curious. He's always looking around, and he always seems to be wondering about what's going on." They wouldn't say curious, though; they would say, "He seems nosy." And I thought to myself, "Nosy? Hmm, I'm not seeing it that way. I think of it as curiosity, and I think of it as a healthy thing, and I'm glad that he's interested in what is going on around him." And after I started reading a little bit more about this, and I heard a speaker talk about curiosity, I realized what a great trait that is to have in a young kid. So many studies have been done about it, and what it means for our happiness.

> When someone (anyone) is asking questions, that's something that we need to nurture and something that we need to develop and guide.

When someone (anyone) is asking questions, that's something that we need to nurture and something that we need to develop and guide, so that they can learn more about the universe. We pay attention to the unfamiliar because it grabs our attention.

But curiosity is about how we pay attention to what's happening in the present. You can think about the future and you can think about the past, but when you're curious and you're asking questions, it's because of what you're thinking about at that very moment.

One author whose work really influenced my research is Susan Engels, PhD, who has studied this topic extensively, including the effects of curiosity on kids in schools. One of her books is *The End of the Rainbow,* and the other one is *The Hungry Mind.* She explains that the more we nurture curiosity when kids are younger, nurturing and developing that curiosity, the more they are likely to go on and continue to practice that trait. And everyone's going to be better for it. We're going to be better for it at work, we're going to be better for it at home, and that person that you're guiding is going to be better for it. Our experiences are richer because of our curiosity.

It all starts with kids and curiosity. In Susan Engels' book, *The Hungry Mind,* she writes about how curiosity can be encouraged at school. These same concepts can apply to people at work and in your home life as well. The need to resolve uncertainty or explain the unexpected is basically what curiosity is, right? Kids use patterns to recognize things and try to make sense out of them. And they ask questions. Curiosity is the reason they ask why and how, and why they start exploring their environment. When we see them doing just that, it's a positive thing.

> Curiosity is the most powerful tool for getting someone to learn something.

Curiosity is the most powerful tool for getting someone to learn something. The kid asking the question at home, at school, around you: it is because they're wondering about something. And if they are wondering about it, they're going to learn it quicker. They're going to remember it longer, and they're going to learn it deeper. Think about that. That's why some people can retain obscure information for years—they are curious about that topic. And they will remember facts about it for longer; much longer. I'm sure you can think of people in your life that demonstrate this.

Have you ever had a conversation with someone and asked them what they thought about a topic you had previously discussed? You were hoping to get their impressions after some time had passed, and they simply can't even remember the details of your discussion. Maybe they were distracted during the initial conversation. Maybe they were multitasking. Maybe they don't even remember having the discussion. Maybe they simply didn't care about the topic at all, and it left their mind the minute the conversation was over (or during ☹).

But conversely, you could be talking with that same person, discussing an event that happened 20 or 30 years ago, and they still remember details about it that are striking, like the final few minutes of a game, what the weather was like, or what they were wearing, etc. That's because they were interested in and cared deeply about that event. Now, years later, because of their deep interest in that event, they can remember SO much about it. That's curiosity at its finest! **This is what we want and need for our planet!**

Our planet needs people who care passionately about topics and are experts in what they love and what they know about. Because those people can, and want to, share that information, passionately. And our teams, our companies, and our families are going to be better for it. Their curiosity changes the world. It's all about what grabs your attention, and then going and finding out more about it.

It just so happens that, in addition to curiosity, kids are influenced by role models (obviously) and encouragement and security. Susan says, "If you're nervous about your environment, and you're feeling insecure in it, you're much less likely to experience curiosity because it's risky." So, for those kids who are in a family, a classroom, or in a university, whether young or old, and they're not feeling secure about asking a question—they're pausing and they're just feeling a little bit intimidated—they're not going to be as curious. They're less likely to ask questions, and they're not going to experience that drive and that, "Wow, I wonder…" feeling.

That sense of wonder comes through when they're curious, but they're not going to be able to experience that when they are feeling at risk. That's a really important point because it goes back to our work life, too. If someone on your team—either someone that you are mentoring or someone who reports to you—is feeling like they can't ask questions because it's risky or they're feeling insecure about it, they're going to feel stifled. And who can benefit from being or feeling stifled? Who can be creative when they're feeling insecure or suppressed? And, if *you* are insecure, you aren't going to be comfortable asking questions.

Another way to destroy curiosity is to put a time frame on it and say, "Go learn about it, but you have half an hour. Find out all you can and then report back to everyone." That puts the pressure of a task and a deadline as the goal rather than gathering information to satisfy curiosity. The wonder that you were experiencing before the restrictions gets squashed.

As I was thinking about this concept of squashing curiosity, I was thinking about the impact on our lives at work and home. Why don't we just ask people more questions? Why don't we ask our teams or family members, "What's the one thing you want to learn more about?" And then encourage them to go do it? Doing this is going to spark interest, it's going to spark creativity, it's going to spark excitement, and then everyone around you is going to feel that. They're going to want to learn more about your topic because you are excited to talk about it. That excitement is contagious. How could this not nurture the relationships on your team and family and get others excited about discovering and creating more ideas for other people, too?

Another great point that I love from Susan Engels' research is, "People who feel an eagerness to learn are happier, less stressed, and healthier." When you're eager to learn, you're curious. That's just the science. You're excited about things that are going on, and how could that not be good for your body and your health, and your mind, too?

A study cited in another book on curiosity, *The Curious: The Desire to Know and Why Your Future Depends On It,* was done by a scientist at the National Institute of Child Health and Human Development in Maryland. He recently discovered something extraordinary. The more actively a baby explores his/her environment, the more likely it is that he/she will go on to achieve academic success as an adolescent.

When I think back to the story about my older son and how curious he was, I find it interesting because he was academically successful. He's a good student, he's a curious person, he likes to learn, and when he's excited about something, he learns it even deeper and goes on and finds even more information about whatever it is. It's wonderful to see. And when I think back to the toddler that he was, I can understand that's exactly what happened. He was always wondering about what was going on, asking a ton of questions. Parents and bosses - never stop nurturing that curiosity!

The research in this book further states that although, as they grow older, most children become more independent of adults, as far as curiosity goes, adults become more important to children as times goes by. This is important to note because if you're nurturing their curiosity when they're younger, great. But as they get older, while they may continue to want to ask questions, if they're not being encouraged to do so by the adults around them, whether it's their teachers, their bosses, their parents, etc., they're probably not going to continue on the path of curiosity and wonderment.

Asking questions is easy, right? Obviously, if you are a curious person and you want to know something about a topic, you'll ask questions. It's an important skill to have, but you need to make sure that these three components are involved. First, you have to know what you don't know. If you ask a question, it's because you're wondering about it, right? You're wondering, "How does this work? Can I learn more about this?" But you have to think about the information you are lacking so you can ask the **right** questions, right?

Second, you have to be able to imagine that there may be several different answers or different scenarios, and then there may be competing possibilities. So, you'll ask the question and then consider the options: "Well, what does this person think about that? What does this resource say about this?" Obviously, we can go onto the internet and find lots of different answers to different questions, but you have to be open to a whole variety of possibilities when you're curious about a topic.

Third, you have to understand that you can learn from other people. We can go onto the internet, and we can ask questions, and we can see what other people or other experts know about that topic, but we need to realize that there is a lot that we can learn from other people. Many different people will have shared information on the internet on any given topic, and there are books and articles and research and blogs. But then also, there are interviews and podcasts, for example. There's always something more to learn. Even if a person isn't necessarily an expert in that topic, you can still ask their opinion on it and learn something.

> We need to realize that there is a lot that we can learn from other people.

My husband and my older son are big fans of Neil deGrasse Tyson, who is this really cool scientist with a great sense of humor. They went to hear him speak, and I don't think they were prepared for him to be as entertaining as he was. But it turns out he's super funny and charismatic, and an excellent speaker. He was on stage talking about science and how great it is, and, of course, because he is a scientist, he thinks that everyone should love science, right?

My husband described how someone stood up at the end of the talk, and asked, "So, science is great and we need it, etc.… but does it really apply to *everything* we're doing, and how important is it, really? What does it really have to do with **everything**?" And Neil, being a funny guy, was really relaxed, and he just said, "Well, let me just give you an example..." (to illustrate how science applies to **everything**). He continued to explain that decades ago, scientists discovered a molecule or atom or something in space (I know, I should know exactly what it was, but for this explanation, the **thing** they discovered is not vital). Scientists discovered something in space, and it seemed pretty cool, but also pretty insignificant. It was one of those things where they thought, "Alright, let's just see where this goes." Eventually, a scientist started asking more questions about this mystery space particle that they found.

It turns out that decades later, this particular, seemingly insignificant, teeny tiny atom or molecule that had been discovered became part of the technology that created magnetic resonance imaging—the MRI machine that diagnoses problems and diseases for millions of people around the world every day! The MRI you guys!

The entire audience was rather astounded about this one little, tiny thing discovered in space years and years ago, that seemed to have no consequence or significance at the time. And then years later, someone took another look at it and continued to ask questions about it—was curious about it—and studied it, and that particular technology resulted in the MRI. This is what curiosity can do!

People! An MRI, that diagnoses health problems and tumors, back problems, shoulders issues—you name it. It finds big and small issues that go on in your body that you need to know about so that physicians can help you! This amazing technology exists all because there was a discovery years ago and someone kept asking questions. Without curiosity and without questions, we wouldn't have that technology today! Just imagine all of the things we wouldn't have if people stopped asking questions.

In the book, *Curiosity,* author Ian Leslie writes, "A society that values order above all else will seek to suppress curiosity, but a society that believes in progress, innovation, and creativity will cultivate that, recognizing that the inquiring minds of its people constitute its most valuable asset." Ian also writes, "The truly curious will be increasingly in demand. Employers are looking for people who can do more than follow procedures competently or respond to requests. Who have a strong interest and desire to learn, solve problems, and ask penetrating questions."

This corresponds with a growth mindset. When I was attending a workshop recently, someone in the audience asked the business leader, "When hiring, what's one of the most important things you look for?" And the speaker replied, "I want people to be lifelong learners. I want people to have a growth mindset. I want people to be curious about things." I remember specifically because I wrote this down. This is what leaders look for in business and in life! We want people to be open to possibilities and questions and to discovering things. Those are the kind of people we want to hire and employ (and work with). And frankly, these are the types of people we want to have in our lives.

Ian Leslie comments, "Computers are smart, but no computer however sophisticated can yet be said to be curious." Obviously, we need computers, and we need technology to solve problems so we can help people with their health and in their lives and in their companies, but computers aren't asking questions, are they? Regardless of whether you can use a computer to figure out these things, the bottom line is that a human being is actually initiating the questions, and that is what triggers the technology to solve the problem.

In *Curious*, Ian writes, "The most fundamental reason to choose curiosity is so we can do better at school or at work. The true beauty of learning stuff, even apparently useless stuff, is that it takes us out of ourselves

Regardless of whether you can use a computer to figure out these things, the bottom line is that a human being is actually initiating the questions, and that is what triggers the technology to solve the problem.

and reminds us that we are part of a far greater project, one that's been underway for at least as long as human beings have been talking to each other." When you're curious, it takes you out of your everyday realm of thinking, and it requires you to explore other possibilities and wonder about the world and people.

This next quote is also from the same book, *Curious, The Desire to Know*: "The more we know about something, the more intense our curiosity is about what we don't know. The intensity of our curiosity is affected by whether we think the information that we're missing is likely to provide insight." So, we're more curious if we think that what we're about to discover can provide insight into our lives. Bingo!

The author also talks about the power of questions and how curiosity requires an edge of uncertainty to thrive. You have to be a little uncertain about things for curiosity to thrive, but if you have too much uncertainty about something, your curiosity freezes. It goes back to that study about insecurity. If people feel insecure, or they're in a home environment that doesn't foster questions and they feel threatened, or if at work you're afraid that if you ask the wrong questions it's not going to be good for you or your team, or it's not encouraged, curiosity cannot thrive. And frankly, you're not going to have that growth mindset, because you're going to be afraid to ask questions and wonder.

Socially, how does curiosity apply to us? People who are curious are more comfortable in a variety of different social scenarios. The more curious people are, the more comfortable they are interacting with strangers, and the more comfortable they are after those interactions. Both the person that's curious and the person they're talking to are going to benefit from the conversation. People enjoy having conversations with curious people because they're asking questions. But it's not just about asking questions, it's being interested in the other person that you're talking to, whether it's your boss, your teammate, or someone that you're getting coffee from.

You know how sometimes you can walk away from an interaction and feel really good, and think, "Gosh, I really liked that person," or, "I got a good feeling from that person." It's almost always because that person was asking questions and displaying interest in you. Do a little experiment for the next couple of days and see what happens: you'll see what I mean. When you leave a conversation or an interaction, whether you're at a store or at work, and you feel really good, it's usually because someone connected with you and then asked you a question. Even if it was just, "How's it going today?", you think, "Wow, that was sweet—that person didn't have to ask me that question." You're leaving that interaction feeling better, and usually it's because you have their undivided attention.

> It's almost always because that person was asking questions and displaying interest in you.

Socially, curious people have all of the following traits. They display a wide range of interests; they're enthusiastic, animated, talkative; they dominate in conversation because they're wondering and expressing ideas and asking questions; and they're interested. We've all been around those people. Those are the people that you want to have around you and on your team, in your families, because you can interact with them and collaborate with them.

And then, without realizing it, when you're around curious people, both strangers and family and friends, you start to display the same qualities. It's not a fluke. Just think about all these great qualities that come about when you're asking questions! So why not be curious, right?

Another really fascinating research study by Gallop was written about in the book, *Curious*, by Todd Kashdan. In this study, more than 130,000 people in more than 130 nations were surveyed—this sample was designed to reflect 96 percent of the Earth's population! Quite a lot, I'm sure you'll agree. They asked people how much enjoyment they experienced on a given day and how that contributed to their happiness. (https://www.awpnow.com/main/2016/02/24/the-power-of-curiosity-chapter-2/)

The results were interesting. "Two factors that influence how much enjoyment a person experiences on a given day were being able to **count on someone for help** and **learning something new yesterday**." So, think about this: you wake up today and you're feeling positive and you're feeling great and you have lots of energy. According to this research, your good mood is because you learned something new the day before and were able to count on someone for help. So, being able to go to people—whether it's your friends, your family, your boss, or your coworkers— and get the help or assistance that you need, is so very important. It's one of the top factors contributing to your happiness.

Remember that Neil deGrasse Tyson seminar that my son and husband attended? When they came home that night and all the next day, they were beaming because of all the information they acquired and the energy about what they learned: how cool it was, the interactions with people there, what a fascinating speaker he was, and how open he was to hearing everyone's questions. That's not an accident! They were so excited to be able to experience that and learn all this cool, new stuff that they could then share with other people. They were experiencing curiosity on so many levels. And it was contagious!

Each day, I look forward to learning something. I tell myself: I'm going to talk to someone new, I'm going to check out this workshop, read this article, or talk to this person about research they've done, and learn something new, and then apply it to what I'm doing in my everyday life. How fascinating it is that the two factors that influence how much enjoyment a person experiences are being able to **count on someone** and **learning something new**. Every day, wherever you're interacting with people, anytime you can learn something new you're just going to get more enjoyment out of life. And, thankfully, this doesn't cost any money!

Author Todd Kashdan also wrote that the keys to a happy life are in developing relationships, growing as a person, and seeking out the new—the new experience, the new information, the new article, the new book, the new movie. What you learn from those experiences—whether you listen to a book or read it, see a movie, have a conversation with someone you haven't met before, or talk with someone you know about a new topic—is the key to being a happy person. Developing those relationships is so important, and you can really only do that when you're asking questions and being inquisitive and wondering about people. Again, this is free.

We are all learning every day, and we're ultimately better people for discovering new things, and sharing with our teams or any of the people we spend time with. Everyone around you is going to benefit from your curiosity. The people that you live with are going to notice because you are going to be a bit more excited, as well as happier, and the people you work with are going to notice because you are going to be contributing more. So, go be curious and ask questions. Never stop asking them and

Never stop asking them and encourage everyone around you to do the same.

encourage everyone around you to do the same. Encourage your kids, encourage the people you live with, and encourage your teammates. Our planet will improve because of it.

Curiosity is the secret that works like a catalyst around creating the life you want. When you're curious about every day, and can stay curious when you're tackling any problem, you can solve it easier. Curiosity breeds creativity. When you are asking questions about your life and the people around you, we all benefit.

5

·····

Joy

(And how to create more of it)

When I started college, I was 17. I had always dreamed of going to school in Chicago. I loved the city—the energy, the excitement, the possibilities. I'm sure it's no surprise that when I arrived, with my 17-year-old self, it was not what I expected.

For starters, I was **only** 17. So, duh. Of course, it wasn't what I expected. And I was broke. I couldn't afford to go to nice restaurants, I didn't have my own car, and I wasn't 21, so going to bars wasn't in the cards (and even if I could get in, I couldn't afford to be there). I used any student loans I had to live and eat and had no help from my parents. This was 1987, so the internet didn't even exist. I couldn't simply call them and ask them to put some money in my account. And, even if I could have asked, no help was coming from my parents. I was on my own (literally and figuratively.)

Even though my circumstances were less than ideal, I was indeed independent and able to spend my time as I wished (when I didn't have to go to class and do homework). So I roamed around the city in my 80's, Chicago Blackhawks jacket and black leggings, with my keys and wallet in one pocket and my mace in the other pocket, dreaming of what it would be like to go into all of the beautiful restaurants someday. I felt joy every time I imagined what was possible in the city. I felt joy walking around the city, thinking about how many cool places there were to visit. I loved seeing people living life and was excited to begin living mine. I chose to see the joy everywhere I went. And I wanted more!

Fast forward 30 years, and I'm finally living in downtown Chicago, enjoying the many experiences I was longing to have, and it's very **joyful**! Yes, joy is what I'm experiencing.

I get to roam the streets now in really comfortable shoes, better clothes, and money in my wallet. I make reservations at the restaurants I want to visit and buy the food I want to eat. It's very similar to the joy I felt at 17. Except now I have more wisdom and perspective. And I cherish it more. Wow, what a difference 30 years can make!

My point is that, both at 17 and again later in my life, I knew I'd experience joy in the city. When I was younger, I did things I could afford, and now that I can afford to have more of the experiences I once craved as a teenager, it's blissful. I am taking in every moment, appreciating all of the life, experiences, and people the city has to offer. I live in a beautiful high rise in the city. I get to sit on our balcony every day and take in amazing views of the sunset (yes, amazing is the word that fits best here).

I recently took a walk by my old high-rise dorm that I stayed in when I was 17. I met some wonderful people there from all around the world. I didn't have any guidance or support, but I made the best of it. I was where I chose to be—I had a dream, and I made it happen. And now, as I walk by there 33 years later, I see some of the same places that I once dreamt of going in, and I'm very grateful that any joy I'd like to experience, I can have. I just need to decide.

What if you could create and experience more joy every day with simple things, at work and at home? What if you just needed to decide. Yes, it's called work for a reason, but why can't there be JOY there, every day? First, let's make sure we're all on the same page. There is a difference between happiness and joy:

"Happiness is tied to circumstances and joyfulness is tied to spirit and gratitude" (*The Gifts of Imperfection* by Brenee Brown). And, according to the Random House dictionary, *joy* means, 'The emotion of great delight or happiness caused by something good or satisfying.'" And finally, **"When people go to work, they shouldn't have to leave their hearts at home."** - Betty Bender.

Betty Bender's quote especially caught my eye because I was often told, when looking for a new job or role, "it's work, it's not supposed to be fun." Or the ever popular, "It's called work for a reason." Okay, okay, I get it. It's work. But I could never settle for that answer. If we're going to spend eight hours a day (and usually more), five days a week at work, for decades, no less, shouldn't we be striving for joy? It just didn't seem right to devote the largest portion of our life not feeling happy or joyful. Who would want to do that? And what kind of society would we have if no one found joy in their work or at work? I shudder to think of what our world would look like.

> And what kind of society would we have if no one found joy in their work or at work?

Unfortunately, I think it's one of the main reasons we have so much road rage and missed/sick time at work, why our society is so unhealthy, and our drug companies are making more than ever on drugs to make us less depressed and anxious. We get up in the morning, get ready for our miserable (or slightly miserable) job, get into the car to ride in traffic, spend eight-plus hours at the office, commute back home in horrible traffic, and then spend the evening complaining about our miserable job to our poor family members. Then we wonder why we feel depressed and anxious, wanting to binge-watch Netflix for the rest of the night.

Think about what a difference it would make if we could feel joyful getting into our car, listening to music that would make us feel happy, hear a podcast that lifted us up, or listen to a book that brought us joy, or taught us about our hobby. Imagine the possibilities! Do you think you would arrive at the office feeling a little happier and smiling more? Do you think you would be less annoyed with traffic? I'm guessing the answer is YES!

What if you could transfer that joy to the office or to your home? What if you could walk into your space, look at a beautiful plant or some pretty flowers on your desk? How about a lovely picture of your family or pets to glance at every few minutes? And then a favorite quote to come back to when you're feeling stressed? Ah, just writing that makes me feel calmer.

I recently purchased a new mouse pad that had a picture of the ocean with a dock, and a wonderful quote on it. Every time I glance down at my mouse or mouse pad, I see this beautiful scene and it makes me smile. Do you think that transfers to the work I'm doing? You bet it does!

There are so many of these little things you can do to bring more joy into your day. They aren't expensive and they take minutes to implement. So, what are you waiting for? Bring a few of these things into your office tomorrow (put them in your home office) and watch your energy transform. I'm going to share my top four favorite ways to create joy at work (or your home, or in any environment). I've adapted these methods from an article about creating more joy in schools.

http://www.ascd.org/publications/educational-leadership/sept08/vol66/num01/Joy-in-School.aspx by Steven Wolk

JOY 1: Find the pleasing things at work or at home!

Whether you consider yourself a lifelong learner or not, whether you loathed school or couldn't wait to do your homework, there is something, maybe several somethings, you love to learn about. For some, it might be cars. For others, it might be the universe or history. For me, it's decorating and creating beautiful things for my home. Whether it's a serious subject or a frivolous one, you can find pleasure in learning about something. (This is the key when you're trying to get your kids to love reading, though I didn't start loving it until I completed my college degrees, and it wasn't required anymore. Go figure!) Take the clues you've been noticing all your life and then go learn more about something that piques your interest.

> Take the clues you've been noticing all your life and then go learn more about something that piques your interest.

How does this apply to work and home? If you can find the pleasing things you would like to learn more about, you will be inspired to learn more, to create more, to work more on those things. And that transfers to your everyday work. It opens up your mind to new possibilities. You feel more positive and excited. And then you start to notice more pleasing things around you. Don't believe me? Try it today. Go read or learn about something you love (in a book, online, on TV), and see if that doesn't spark some ideas for you...ideas about work, your home, your love life, your kids, or your next adventure. I guarantee it will!

Inspiration is addictive. When you're regularly inspired, you want more of that feeling, and you seek it out. You want to find and see more pleasing things all around you. If you work in an office (whether at home or somewhere else), make that office more pleasing. Bring pictures of your favorite things to work. Buy an inexpensive bulletin board and alternate your favorite pictures and quotes on it. Get rid of anything on your desk that annoys you or stresses you and bring in some items that make you smile. Buy some flowers each week to look at every day.

Make your work or home space as inviting as you can. Change things around so that all day long you can see something that makes you smile. Focusing on what you really like will keep your mood up and give you more inspiration to create! For example, I love walking into my office and seeing the sun coming up over the lake and the beautiful buildings surrounding the city. The view is spectacular, and it always brings me joy to see it. I move around during the day to take in the different views, enjoying more light when I need it. Why sit in the same seat all day long? You have a choice!

> Change things around so that all day long you can see something that makes you smile.

When you work at home, light some candles with your favorite scent. Keep your favorite gum or mints on your desk. Print some pictures from your phone and frame them. Take images or quotes of people you admire and hang them where you can see them every day. It sounds simple. It is simple. But those few simple things will spark joy every day for you, and anyone and everyone around you will benefit. The more positive and joyful you can feel, the more of that energy you will bring forth into your conversations, your emails, and your work—and people will notice. But most importantly, you'll notice, and you'll want more of it!

JOY 2: Create choices at work and at home!

Do you remember being in second grade? Do you remember those little reading circles where you could sit on the mat and pick your favorite book to read? Or when you had free drawing time or talking time when the teacher gave you a break from learning? Hopefully, you loved that time. If you did, it's likely because you were able to choose something **you** wanted to do. It was "free time." As adults, we still always wish we had more "free time."

Free time, to me, means time to do whatever we wish. We can read, nap, watch TV, take a drive, lounge, browse online, or walk around our favorite store. It's about doing whatever you wish to do with your time. Well, that's what I'm talking about with this option. Create choices at work.

I know some work (and home) environments are more restrictive than others. Some jobs don't lend themselves to many variables. I get that. What I'm suggesting is to create choices wherever possible. For example, you show up to work and put your things down/away, in a cabinet, drawer, etc. Are you throwing them somewhere or are you placing them on a hook nearby? Do you have a place for those things so you can look at an uncluttered surface while you work? Find a way to keep those things organized so your brain can focus.

Another example is to decide what order your actual tasks are going to be done. Depending on your responsibilities, it's likely that you have certain things that have to be done by the end of the day. You can choose to do those things first, second, or last, as long as they get done. That's your **choice**! Usually, you can assert some independence over how and when you'll do the necessary tasks. We're all more productive at different times of the day. Find out what works best and design your day as you choose. While you're choosing when you do your tasks, maybe you can choose where you do them and move around your home or office and take in different views as you work. Most offices have large common areas that are barely used and safe to work in. Mix it up and choose where you're working.

What about when you take breaks or eat lunch? These are also often choices. If you're fortunate and get to choose, you are deciding when you need a break. Maybe on one day you'd like to go to

70   JULIE BRUNS

lunch earlier because you're hungry; and the next day, you decide to go later, to avoid the lunch crowd. Take your break and go outside whenever you can for some fresh air or exercise. Read an interesting article while you're there. These are **choices** that you get to control. And you should. Maybe you're going to work on a certain task until it gets done so you can get it off your plate, then go on a break to reward yourself. That is a choice you get to make. Choices!

> Creating choices wherever and whenever you can will help you feel more joyful because you are deciding how to design your day.

Creating choices wherever and whenever you can will help you feel more joyful because you are deciding how to design your day. You are creating the type of day you would like to have, regardless of the things you have to do. All of these little choices add up to you having control over your happiness and your joy. Help your kids and your teams implement these choices whenever possible.

If, on the other hand, your choices are limited at work (or home), and your day is very structured, you can create choices in other areas of your life. You can decide what type of car you drive, what music or news you listen to on the way, what radio interviews or podcasts you hear before you start work, etc. And the same applies for your commute home. If you're not driving, then you're walking or taking public transportation, and you can control all of those things from your phone. You have complete control over what goes into your brain, your mind, and your body. Use that time to make it count! And that will flow over into your workday, I promise.

JOY 3: Create things at work and at home!

Creating things at work might sound unattainable, depending on your role/job/environment. Maybe you are in finance and you create spreadsheets all day. I have to say, this is my worst nightmare, which is why I'm not in finance. But I know that for some, this is heaven. I use this example because I want to point out that no matter what your tasks are, you are still creating. You can create those spreadsheets with your choice of font type, size, and color. You can highlight, format text and dates, and create formulas. See what I mean? Choices (even in spreadsheets)! This is the same concept if you work at home. You can be creative with any task you have to finish.

My business is learning and development, and I create presentations, articles, and podcasts. I'm creating PDFs, emails, and website pages. I have lots of tasks I can complete to spark ideas and create beauty. I get to decide what they look like each time. And even think outside the box a little. Just because something has always been done a certain way, doesn't mean it has to continue.

> Just because something has always been done a certain way, doesn't mean it has to continue.

a certain way, doesn't mean it has to continue. Often you'll find that 'the way it's always been done' is because the person completing that task didn't have time to consider another way, or simply never thought of doing it differently. When you suggest process improvements, more often than not you'll hear, "Sure, give it a try." So, go ahead!

Maybe you can't create much in the work you're doing, but you can create your environment, the items you look at, the way things are arranged, the colors you see each day, the text you view, etc. Maybe you have an idea to create more beauty in your common work areas. Ask your manager if she/he would be willing to let you try something that others can benefit from. Maybe you can create a quote of the day to post where people gather frequently. Perhaps this is something you can do digitally and send it out to the company each day – a positive quote to get their day started off in a great direction. It doesn't have to be a big thing. Creating any little thing will get your artistic juices flowing and give you more ideas.

Finally, I'd like to remind you: even if you don't consider yourself a creative person, you have ideas. Everyone does. Maybe you're thinking that your idea might not be good—but who's to say it isn't? Try something little and see what happens. Do this at home first if that makes it easier. In the end, you'll be proud of yourself for trying—and it will likely be received well. If it isn't, try something else. Don't stop trying. **Think about all the things we wouldn't have if people stopped trying. Go create!**

JOY 4: Celebrate achievements at work and at home!

This one is big! Can you celebrate your own achievements? Of course, you can! You might be thinking, but Julie, I'm not a manager. I don't have a job where I can be recognized or recognize others. Whether you are a stay-at-home mom, a CEO, or some-where in between, you can indeed celebrate achievements at work or at home, anytime. And it doesn't have to cost any money at all.

We often get so busy moving from task to meeting, etc., that we forget about what we've accomplished. Take a few moments to celebrate the good results you have achieved, the meeting that went well, or the training session/project that you received compliments about. And when you do get a compliment, ask yourself or someone who was there, what did they think went well or what did they like about it? Getting these specific details will help you create more ways to accomplish these same results the next time.

It only takes a minute to ask, "What specifically did you like about it?" And people are usually happy to share.

One way to achieve celebrating personally is to compose a draft email (without a recipient) and start listing all of your accomplishments. Add to it when you think of a new one. I bet you'll have a long list, and you can go look at it any time. A second way is to keep any compliments and thank-you notes you receive from others in an email folder called "Reminders." Any time you're having a crappy day, just go into this folder and look at the great notes you've received. Simple and free! Try it!

Giving praise is as important as receiving it. When acknowledging others, start with the smallest and easiest way to celebrate accomplishments. You can write a note on the refrigerator recognizing someone in your family for something they achieved. Did they finally make their bed

> Giving praise is as important as receiving it.

like you've been asking them to all week? Celebrate them! Did they fold the laundry beautifully and put it away just like you've been showing them? Celebrate them! Just grab a post-it note and put it in their room or on the bathroom mirror. They'll love it!

At work, whether you are a manager with many direct reports or a recent college graduate who is newly employed, you can celebrate anyone. Did you have a recent meeting with someone who had a great idea? Tell them so during or after the meeting. Have you been on several calls with a team member who is always positive and has great questions? Tell them so (in person and via email). Have you noticed someone at work who is always extremely helpful and great to work with? Tell them so, and more significantly, write an email to their manager, telling them what you appreciate about that team member. Who doesn't love a sincere compliment?

These options take just a few minutes, cost no money, and will make someone's day. And, if you've never thought about it before, it will make your day too. How? Celebrating someone's achievements, big or small, will bring your energy up. You're brightening someone's day, you are appreciating them, recognizing their efforts, and then telling someone else about them as well. You are spreading the love. We all want to be recognized and celebrated. This basic human need is universal. We want to know that what we're doing matters. We want to help others and be appreciated for it. Try this for a week. Celebrate someone's achievement every day, in any little way you can. Then see if you don't want to continue doing it.

Joy cannot be obtained without your permission. This secret will change your life, but you have to be intentional about it. Ask yourself what joy feels like. Ask yourself what joy looks like. It's different for each of us, which is the best part. Joy could be sipping your morning coffee after you exercise. Joy could be laying under the sheets for an extra half hour before you slip out of bed. Discover whatever joy is for you, and then do more of it! Every single day.

6

. . . . .

Resilience

(It builds character)

No one goes through life without setbacks. Not one single person. I began my journey over 50 years ago, born into a family as 1 of 11 children, with 8 girls and 3 boys under 1 roof, with four bedrooms and 2.5 baths, complete with two parents struggling to make ends meet (along with a plethora of other struggles). You can probably guess why they were struggling. Who can really comprehend having that many kids while NOT struggling? Although, sometimes I do meet big families who aren't struggling financially, have loving relationships, have everything they need and are prospering. What's the difference?

I've spent my life asking this question. I think I may have finally found the answer.

> I've spent my life asking this question. I think I may have finally found the answer.

As a young girl, I came to these realizations: having a big family is stressful. Having a big family is expensive. Having a big family is a problem. Having a big family is a burden. I concluded early on that the more I could do for myself, the less of a burden I would be. And so, off I went making good friends (with good families), doing well in school, completing all of my chores well, joining clubs and sports, and earning money. I was good at getting along with people and knew how to blend in and follow the rules. I would not be a problem!

I needed to learn how to get where I wanted to go on my own, and I was building resilience. Ah, resilience – what is it actually? I like to define what we're talking about with a simple definition because sometimes a certain word means something different to each person, so I thought I'd start with this definition of resilience from Webster's Dictionary. **Resilience**: "The capacity to be able to recover quickly from difficulties and toughness. The ability of a substance or an object to spring back into shape or elasticity." Resilience is the capacity to recover quickly from difficulties; toughness.

I was building resilience, but I wasn't mindful of this at my young age. I was always trying to learn the best way to get what I wanted. I wanted to learn how to be better and smarter, the quickest way possible. It's probably nothing new to realize you cannot get to wisdom and insight without pain and suffering. We all want to get past just surviving and existing and get to that place where we can be wise and courageous, and we can thrive! And we get there by experiencing adversity and discovering just how strong we are.

Incidentally, this is also the way we obtain self-esteem. We're not given self-esteem. We earn self-esteem. This is an especially important concept, so I want to say it another way. Growing up, I'd hear people say, "I have low self-esteem." Usually it was girls saying these things (not surprising, I'm sure). I concluded it meant they didn't think very highly of themselves. But I was smart and competent, and I earned self-esteem because I performed tasks that I was proud to perform. I was resilient and figured things out. I asked questions, and if I couldn't do something, I learned how.

Not everything is easy to learn, and we're not good at every-thing we do, even if we can learn how to do it. That's just life. But we can't help to shape someone else's self-esteem. That comes from within. We build our own self-esteem. Tackling tough issues and coming out on the other side? That builds self-esteem. Trying something you don't know how to do, then completing it? That builds self-esteem. Building self-esteem builds resilience.

The more I researched resilience, the more I realized, "This is me! I am very resilient." When I was a teenager and I would tell my woes to my older sister, Sue, she would always say, "That builds character." If a boy that I liked didn't like me back, "That builds character." If I were disappointed that I couldn't go to a certain event because I didn't have the money, "That builds character." If a friend had betrayed my trust, "That builds character." This phrase would come up a lot over the years, especially in high school and college. Along the way, as more woes would come along, we started to joke about it. We wondered, when exactly do you have *enough* character? It seemed to me and my sister Sue that if you are "building it" as you go, then you'd have enough after a while, and you'd be good to go. Your character would be "built," and you'd be strong enough to face anything. Period. But that's not how life works.

We all know someone who has bounced back from problems, whether it's a difficult childhood, an accident, a misfortune, or all of the above. I think we can all agree that bouncing back stories are inspirational. There are countless books and movies telling stories about regular and famous people bouncing back. Stories like the underdog who was told they couldn't do something or the little girl that had an idea that no one believed was possible. We see it all the time. And we want more! We want to know: how did they do that? What help did they have? And, most importantly for me, can they teach me how?

Bouncing back—being resilient—really is the key to being joyful and happy in your life. Eventually, everyone's going to face something that doesn't turn out the way they want it to. If you think about those people that have achieved a level of success that you admire or are doing things that you respect or have a positive attitude you appreciate, it's almost always because they came through something that was really tough; they came out the other side, they learned lessons from it, and they bounced back from it. They are resilient!

During my research, I came across this great book called *Resilience* by Eric Greitens, a retired Navy Seal. It is hard-won wisdom for living a better life, and it's a really cool book about the author's own life. In this book, he's writing letters to a friend, a fellow veteran, who's having some issues and dealing with some real hardships. His intention was to help his friend get through it all and help him feel better. Eric started reflecting more on how we get to where we are and how we bounce back from things that are tough on us. Sometimes it might take a week or two to recover, or sometimes it might take years. You probably know someone that just hasn't bounced back from a hardship.

As he talks to this friend in these letters, Eric is saying "here's what I think can help you." One of the first things he writes about is why resilience is so important. He shares this quote, "Resilience is the key to a well-lived life. If you want to be happy, you need resilience. If you want to be successful, you need resilience. You need resilience because you can't have happiness, success or anything else without meeting hardship along the way."

No one goes through life without experiencing setbacks or hardships to some degree. Everyone has them. But you can't get past them and get to a better place in your life unless you are resilient; unless you have the tools to say, "I want to be more positive. I want to look at the people that are where I want to be. I want to go get the resources I need to help me through this hard time." This mindset in itself takes resilience.

This skill and mindset take practice. Some people learn it right away, some people learn it later in life, and some people are taught it through parents and school, etc. Everyone comes to it from a different place. The important thing is that you come to it. And the earlier the better. Bouncing back is being resilient, and you can't get to the next level of your life or past the next hardship without it.

In one of the letters to his friend, Eric says, "to move through pain to wisdom, from fear to courage, from suffering to strength requires resilience." You never really gain wisdom without experiencing some pain. *Wisdom* is the result of learning something after you experience it, talk about, reflect on it, and eventually share it. This is why older people have so much of

> *Wisdom* is the result of learning something after you experience it, talk about, reflect on it, and eventually share it.

it. Because the longer you live, the more experiences you have, and consequently, the more wisdom you develop.

Ah, wisdom. If only we had the advantage of having it before we made any tough (or stupid) decisions.

Younger people are often taught resilience by their parents as they're growing up. But some kids didn't really have anyone to teach it to them, and they had to learn resilience through experiencing and surviving hard times. You can't get to being wise, courageous, and strong without pain, fear, or suffering. You simply can't. What does it take to go from a bad place to a good place? What are those skills? What's required for you to get there and feel really good about coming out on the other side? Resilience. When we are resilient, we can turn pain into strength, wisdom, and joy.

Below is a story of resilience: about surviving being laid off from work back in 2009 when the economy tanked!

I'd like to start out by saying that I felt, in my bones, that something was off. I would go home from work and tell my husband, "Something's going on at work." I just had a sense about it. The fact is: we women are *especially* good at this intuition thing.

I think we discredit it a lot of the time because we either think we're being too sensitive, or more importantly, if we're right, we'll have to do something about it. And that takes courage! We may have to sacrifice, compromise, or make a tough decision because we "know" something. Getting it confirmed means we'll probably be uncomfortable for a while. The good news: **being uncomfortable isn't deadly. It's just difficult.**

> When we are resilient, we can turn pain into strength, wisdom, and joy.

It was late in the year, nearly Christmas, and I was still getting a vibe around the office that bad things were brewing. Subsequently, Christmas came and went, and now it was January. It was early morning, and I was working away at my desk. I had been at the office for less than an hour. Unexpectedly, my desk phone rang (remember desk phones?) and it was the senior executive (the one who was avoiding me), and he asked me to come down to his office for a minute. Ugh. There it was…that pit in my stomach. That sinking feeling that something bad was going to happen.

The stories we tell ourselves before we actually know the facts are always worse. We make up stories about things in our heads and come up with the worst-case scenarios. We assume so many details about the situation or the people in the situation. We assume everything. And you know what they say about assuming?

It was a short conversation. "We are laying off ten percent of the staff, and you're one of them. You will get two weeks' severance. You'll need to collect your things now and leave the office." I think I asked why. I think there was an apology somewhere in there, albeit brief. I left the executive's office in shock. I gathered my things and walked out of the building. The entire process, from phone call to walking out the front door, was probably 30 minutes. I was on my way back to the train station that I had just come from a mere two hours earlier, only now with all my belongings in a bag, no longer employed. I thought to myself, "This builds character".

As soon as I left the office, I called a co-worker—my friend—who hadn't arrived at work yet, to tell her what happened. She was shocked, but supportive. We chatted about my feelings that something had been going on leading up to this and about what I thought I would do now. Maybe this was a good thing after all. I just needed to process it. And then I hopped on the train. Homeward bound.

"That which does not kill us makes us stronger" (says the famous German philosopher Friedrich Nietzsche, and Kelly Clarkson for you pop music fans.)

What did I do? I cried for months and lamented about losing my job, telling everyone I knew how unfortunate I was. No, just kidding. (That doesn't build character.) I spent the next several months working out, researching, going to job clubs, volunteering, and deciding what I wanted in my next role. The truth was that I was getting bored in that role, and it had changed. I wanted to find something with lots of variety and new challenges. I had accomplished (and contributed) a ton in my role, but it was time for a change.

While I job hunted, I knew it was important to balance my days with exercise, fresh air, conversations, research, and networking. I knew that sitting in front of the computer for 8 hours a day was not the way to find my next job. So, I didn't do that. I embraced my new freedom. I began researching other jobs and even going back to substitute teaching, until I realized that public education was not where I was ultimately supposed to land. (That took a few months to realize.)

Bouncing back and making the best of it was never NOT an option. I was going to take this circumstance that I had no control over and turn it around. I knew that wallowing in self-pity wasn't going to produce anything positive. And it certainly wasn't going to make anyone want to hire me. I was going to land an awesome job. And I did just that, about 10 months later, working for an awesome company, traveling and meeting some great people that are still in my life today.

The psychologist, Mihaly Csikszentmihalyi, is quoted in the book, *Resilience*: "Of all the virtues we can learn, no trait is more useful, more essential for survival and more likely to improve the quality of life than the ability to transform adversity into an enjoyable talent." This quote says so much about the significance of resilience. There are countless virtues—such as compassion, courage, integrity, etc.—but this one in particular is so important because we want to get past surviving and get to that place where we can be wise and feel courageous. And we really can't get to where we want to be until we get past the adversity. We have to face that challenge, and conquer it. That's when we are resilient. That's also when and how we build self-esteem. We prove to ourselves that we can do something, even if, and especially if, it's tough. We get stronger, we gain confidence, and we continue to be resilient.

In Brenee Brown's book, *The Gifts of Imperfection,* among other topics, she researched how people come to be resilient and what the most common factors are, and I'm sure you won't be surprised to learn these five things she discovered. I'm going to elaborate on them from my perspective.

#1 Resilient people are resourceful. People that are resilient are resourceful and have good problem-solving skills. I'm sure we've all met those people that seem to always be suffering from some kind of minor disaster and are willing to complain about their many problems to anyone who will listen. They have a "woe is me," victim mentality. People like this are not actually trying to solve anything. They just want to complain. Victims are not resilient.

People that are resilient and that really seek to benefit from getting to the other side, where wisdom is—they are resourceful.

They seek out resources that are going to help them solve their problems. But if you weren't born with these skills and no one taught you how to be resourceful, you had to figure it out on your own by telling yourself, "I need to solve this problem." Or, "Who could help me with this problem or that issue?" (A really great book on this topic of problem solving is *Everything is Figureoutable* by Marie Forleo. She really dives into how life's problems, big and small, can almost always be figured out.)

#2 Resilient people are more likely to seek help. Seeking help might seem obvious, but I'm finding in mid-life that most people try to solve their problems on their own for quite a while before they ask for help. I see this with my own children, in people my age, and in people much older than me. I think it's because we're embarrassed that we can't solve the problem on our own. We think we might be judged harshly for having the problem (and not knowing what to do about it). We're sometimes ashamed that we're having the problem at all.

But trying to solve our problems on our own has many disadvantages. It takes us longer, we have more stress, and we can't always see the best path forward with our own mind. Being resilient doesn't mean we have to figure it all out, all the time. It just means that we know we can figure it out and eventually bounce back (with help). And P.S., people who can ask for help and can let others brainstorm with them and offer guidance, are helping those other people to feel purposeful and are also helping to build the other person's resilience! You are giving a gift to those from whom you are receiving help. Think about how good it feels to help someone (whether it's a stranger or someone you know). Think about that feeling you get when you've had compassion for someone, offered a helping hand, or were able to help someone

> Being resilient doesn't mean we have to figure it all out, all the time.

solve a problem, big or small. Doing it all by yourself is robbing others of the joy of helping you. Think about that next time you hesitate to ask for help.

#3 Resilient people believe there is something they can do that will help them to manage their feelings and to cope. They know that there is a solution out there. They have power over their problem, and because they have power over it, they believe it can be conquered.

Ah, believing. This is a big one. Maybe the biggest! Why?

Because if we don't believe something can be resolved, then even though we make strides to solve our problem, we then sabotage the solutions we find because, deep down inside, we don't believe it can be solved. Unfortunately, as a result, this is how the universe responds. And, I know, it's annoying. You're probably thinking, "What? No matter how hard I work, if I don't believe it deep down, it won't happen?"

Yes, hard work is important in anything we do. We must practice, put in the time, make the sacrifices others aren't willing to make, etc. BUT, if we do all that and don't believe that it's going to happen, it won't matter how many hours we put in and how many sacrifices we're making. It cannot happen. That deep-down belief is the THING that decides it all. Just ask people who have succeeded. The ones who bounced back and got stronger. The ones who bounced back and got richer. The ones who bounced back and became successful.

They believed they would get through it. They believed that, with all of the hard work and sacrifices, they could get past "it". It doesn't make a difference what "it" is. The **belief** brings a feeling to your body and mind. That feeling is what helps you conquer the setback (with all of the other hard work, etc.). Our brains are so incredibly powerful. They really can work harder than our hands. We could actually do a little less work bouncing back and get there sooner if we just practiced believing more. How? See my chapters on mindfulness and manifesting.

#4 Resilient people have social support available to them. Whether it's friends or family or strangers, they have people to go to who will support them. They have people to collaborate with. They have people that care about them. They have all of this because they've built it. We can't have a strong support network if we've led a selfish life, only ever looking out for ourselves. We cannot raise children who have a support network if we've taught them to look out only for themselves. We cannot have these resources if we don't have compassion for others. Continue to build your networks, always.

#5. Resilient people are connected with others. Whether you have a close family unit or, maybe, you just have a great group of friends, the bottom line is you're out there connecting to people. (My chapter on connections dives deeper into this.) Those connections, that problem solving, that reaching out - all of those things contribute to being resilient, managing your pain and changing your negative circumstances. You can learn from them, and feel better, and then move on to the next thing that you want to conquer.

> You can learn from them, and feel better, and then move on to the next thing that you want to conquer.

Recently, as I was listening to a radio show, a woman was complaining about a negative experience that she'd had. The host was trying to help her think about it a different way. They spoke about resilience and what someone could do to get out of negative situations. The host suggested some of the things she could do, one of which was to copy healthy behaviors. This method is easier than trying to come up with a solution when you're feeling negative. Sometimes it takes a bigger shift to get out of your negative headspace. And we all know we cannot solve a problem when we're thinking negatively. But maybe trying to copy someone else's healthy behavior will give us just enough personal perspective to feel a little differently about our problem. Sometimes, pretty often, it only takes a slight shift. Copying healthy behaviors will help build resilience.

We've all been there. Someone will try to help us with our problem and say, "Well, you can do this," or, "Did you try this?" And all we can say is, **"No, but..."** or **"Yes, and** it didn't work because...." We whine, whine, whine. Just thinking about how annoying I can be when I'm feeling this way is annoying me now. We can't be creative with that negative mindset. It will serve us best to get out of that mindset as quickly as possible.

Bouncing back is easier if we just do something else entirely. It works best for me if I do the opposite thing. For example, if I'm trying to write and I can't focus, I go for a walk. If I'm trying to read and research, and it seems like I can't find what I need or focus, I walk away from my computer, even for 10 minutes. I get up and complete a brief task, totally unrelated to what I was doing. You get the idea. Switch quickly. Don't loathe what you're doing and go down the unproductive rabbit hole for hours.

It seems counter-intuitive, but resilience is persevering in your desire to keep the momentum going by switching to something else entirely, even just for a few minutes.

This isn't complicated. We can simply choose something else—something else that feels like a better fit. Something that doesn't annoy us. Something that will help get our mind off that other task we're working so hard to accomplish. Resilience isn't always just bouncing right back to complete the task. It's knowing when the task will not get completed, and that even if it does, it won't be what you want. It seems counter-intuitive, but resilience is persevering in your desire to keep the momentum going by switching to something else entirely, even just for a few minutes. Getting out of your head, to a new environment, will usually spark another idea, or at least get you refocused so you can accomplish the task at hand.

To increase resilience, let's get back to copying healthy behaviors. If you're not typically a problem-solving person, you can look at people that are healthier, that are solving problems more regularly and are more positive about them and start thinking about things in a more productive way. If you copy that healthy behavior, it becomes part of who you are, and your responses to things will improve. It's the same concept when you parent. Your kids are much more likely to model your behaviors than follow what you tell them to do.

Practicing positive self-talk also helps with problem solving. People will say, "Well, I don't know if that's going to work." But if you phrase it in a different way and say, "Here's what's going to work instead," or "What *could* work?" and accentuate things that are going well, you're going to get more of the positive effects. I was recently listening to a webinar with a corporate leader. He was about to say something, and then he stopped himself and said, "You know what, I'm not going to say it in a negative way, I'm going to turn it into a positive," and then he commented in a positive way. That's what great leaders do. It's simply spinning it so you can look at it in a healthier way. And with this slight modification, more solutions are going to come. (See my chapter on connections for an example of this.)

Finally, it helps to tell people *exactly how* you got out of that negative place. When you have built resilience, when you have learned through your struggles and you're more courageous and you're wiser, share. Sharing how you achieved that wisdom also helps build even more resilience. You can share your negative experiences, but the important thing to concentrate on is, "How did I get out of that and what skills brought me to this better place in my life?" That's what people want to know, and that's what people need to know so they can be healthier and happier. Share how bouncing back, taking another shot at something you missed, and moving forward, even when you felt negative or scared, has benefited you. It's not something someone can give you. Remember, you don't *get* self-esteem. **You earn self-esteem.** And ultimately, you do it yourself. You do it by being resilient!

Resilience is the secret we're always building and developing. We do this by remembering how we were able to get through something difficult. We are stronger than we know. We can embrace anything and conquer it, but only when we face it. We cannot face what we don't acknowledge. Resilience helps us face things, knowing we can AND WILL come out more powerful on the other side.

7

· · · · ·

Gratitude

(Thankfully, yes!)

Awhile ago I was giving another workshop on gratitude and I wanted to up the ante. I have read a lot about gratitude and its benefits, and, of course, have researched its impact. But this time, I wanted to put my money where my mouth was, so to speak. I wanted to be able to report on the practice of gratitude and how it could indeed give you more. More what? More of whatever you wanted. You see, I'm not sure if you've heard, but what you focus on expands. That's right! If you focus on the negative things, more negative comes your way, or you simply see more negative. If you focus on the good, yep, more good comes your way; you see more good in people, you experience more good, etc. Good begets good. Don't believe me? Try it. I did.

One February day, in the middle of the LONGEST month in the Midwest (because anyone living here knows how long February feels, even though it's the shortest month of the year), I decided that every morning I would say out loud three specific things I was grateful for, before I even got out of bed. Why that way? I wouldn't have to rely on pen and paper, my phone, or anything else to carry out my mission. I just needed my brain, and I'm always carrying that with me. This was the easiest way I could think of, and this method would give me no excuses. Let me back up a second.

I wouldn't have to rely on pen and paper, my phone, or anything else to carry out my mission.

A year before this practice began, I decided to stop watching the news. I really only watched it for 15 minutes each morning (never at night), but that was still too much. I live in Chicago, where there are cold winters, and most homes have basements. If you have a basement, it's great in the summer, because it's very cool indeed! In the winter, though, that's another story. It's always a little cold. So, I would go downstairs (or my husband would sweetly do this) and turn on the portable heater (in addition to our central heat). Once the basement would warm up, I could work comfortably in our home office.

While the basement was warming up, I would watch *The Today Show*. I didn't particularly love watching the news, but I liked the show's energy, and I could take 15 minutes to wake up, warm up, and get ready for work. So, I did that every day for about three years (a big mistake, looking back; I wasted so much time and energy). I'm sure you're not surprised to hear that this did nothing to make me more grateful, unless you count the blessings I would feel when I saw some poor person sharing their news-breaking tragedy. I would silently be grateful that I wasn't in their shoes, then go on with my day. The news would remind me that it could always be worse. This is a low bar.

Sometimes when I was traveling and I watched the news in the morning, I would actually say out loud to myself, "What are you watching this for? This is doing nothing to make your life better." So why watch? Simple: habit. Habits are funny things. We always think it's going to be so hard to create a new habit - a new way of eating, a new way of exercising, a new way of thinking about something, so that we can have or be something a little better. What we don't as easily realize is that all the other little habits we already have are just as powerful. We're already in those habits, so we don't really even think of them anymore. But every habit is powerful because we do them on autopilot. Little or big, when we want to make a change, we have to make a commitment to stop or start something.

I knew this new habit of not watching the news would take more effort if I tried this at home (because of all of those already ingrained habits), so when I was away on a business

> Little or big, when we want to make a change, we have to make a commitment to stop or start something.

trip with my husband and working from the hotel, I decided that instead of watching the news for 15 minutes when I woke up (and I didn't have the excuse of the basement needing to be warmed up), I would go for a walk outside. I did this for three days. It didn't really feel like a sacrifice or a new habit because I was in a new place and couldn't necessarily keep all of my usual routines. And when I came back home, tada! No more morning news. No more depressing stories. No more talking in circles over political issues. No more frustrating conversations when questions weren't getting answered. Oh, and a bonus! No more depressing commercials in between all of that negativity.

I was finally out of that habit. And it only took three days. I've read that it usually takes three weeks to break a habit. I think I discovered a way to accelerate that process. Go on a trip! Put yourself in a different environment for a few days and try something new. Thankfully, I have not watched the news (except for a quick weather report) in over three and a half years. What a relief! I've saved so much time and energy, and now I have a fabulous new habit that has made my life significantly better!

How has this changed my life? Well, for starters, I don't begin my day with depressing news. If you haven't noticed, there aren't very many feel-good stories in the news. And the commercials are almost worse. Why is that? Because the companies that sponsor the news, for example the pharmaceutical companies, know that people watching the news will be more depressed, sad, and anxious, and need their drugs to feel better. This is brilliant if you're a pharmaceutical company.

Second, I get to intentionally choose what I'm going to focus on that day. Rolling over, turning the alarm clock off, then turning on the TV to watch something that either takes our mind off of a problem, helps us avoid getting out of bed, or starts up the anxiety engine, are all things that will hinder our health and wellness. Instead, setting an intention, thinking about what

> I get to intentionally choose what I'm going to focus on that day.

positive thing you'd like to focus on, what you'd like to accomplish, or what you'd like to feel or reveal today: now, that stimulates enthusiasm to get your day going. It's not easy to set positive intentions when mired in negativity that someone else is telling you to worry about.

One more point about starting each day. Waking up to a new day, every day, is a gift. I know that's a major simplification, but it's true. None of us is promised a new day. None of us is guaranteed to have anything on any given day. So, why start our days with stories, people, and things that are going to put us in a negative space, steal our positive outlook, and zap our creativity? Dramatic, maybe. True, definitely.

So now, my gratitude practice has replaced watching the news. I start my day with wonderful feelings about having what I need and want instead of with negative stories and pain. And throughout the day, I am constantly looking for things to be grateful for and to prove to myself how much beauty is out there. And now I see more beauty! Who wouldn't want to have more beauty and less negativity in their lives?

Finally, I have more time on my hands because I don't get sucked into the stories; I don't wait for the commercial to end, and I don't waste that time anymore. And now, with that new time freed up, I fill it with something that will, indeed, make me feel happier, fuller, and more alive. Gratitude is what I fill it with.

Specifically, my practice is this: every morning, as soon as I wake up, before I get out of bed and before I even open my eyes, I say three things I'm grateful for. It could be as simple as: I'm grateful for these soft sheets; I'm grateful for my beautiful bedroom; I'm grateful that I have clothes to wear, no matter what the weather.

I have been doing this for almost 4 years! I do it every morning, and it is truly amazing how many things there are to be grateful for. I think of the sunrise, the nice car I'm about to get in, the full tank of gas, or the myriad of comfortable shoes I can put on my feet, etc.

Why does this small change in my morning routine make such a difference? How does noticing a few random things I already have make me feel different and make my day different? The science around this is simple. Focusing on things to be grateful for will force you to look for them. Throughout the day, you'll find yourself searching for anything to be grateful for. And guess what? You will have more good things happening to you. Because what you focus on expands. What you give your attention to expands. It's the same reason that if you think you will not get a good parking space, you will not find one. If you pull into the parking lot and just know you'll get a great spot, something suddenly opens up, and you have a great spot.

This thought process applies to so many areas of our lives. Even when considering weight loss, gratitude plays an important role. When we decide to lose weight, as soon as we determine that we're going to change the way we eat, what happens? Anyone who has ever tried this will probably agree that the first thing that happens is panic. Oh no! We can't have that ice cream anymore. Or, "I have such a craving for chocolate!" Or fill in the blank for the countless cravings we might have.

This is not some miraculous phenomenon. This is our brain, thinking that the moment we can't have that thing we want, we want it with a vengeance! I think we can all relate to this. No matter how many times we go on a diet, decide to get fit, make a resolution to change our habits, this thought process sets in, and we're doomed before we even start. We focus on NOT being able to have that very thing we want, and it's all we can think about. We start noticing more commercials about ice cream/chocolate/____(fill in the blank). We are focusing more on it, and so we experience more angst about it. Think about it for a second. If you're concentrating on the fact that ice cream is off the table for now, and eating it will keep you from reaching your goal, and you can't have it any longer, etc., how are you going to feel? You're going to want ice cream like crazy! Who wouldn't?

However, there's a trick to feeling better about this! As I've learned, practicing gratitude, and especially in meditation, it's pretty difficult to feel deprived when you're appreciating what you have. Think about a toddler for a minute. Whether you're a parent or not, you've witnessed this in any store on any given day. As soon as you (or that nearby parent) tell them they can't have something (a toy, a cookie, a sucker), they throw a temper tantrum, and it's all they can ask about for the next hour! It's infuriating!

> It's pretty difficult to feel deprived when you're appreciating what you have.

They think if they ask for it enough times, they'll eventually get it. The more you say no, the more they want it, and the harder they cry. From my experience being a parent, I can tell you that in those moments we want to (and sometimes will) say or do anything to stop it and the humiliation we're feeling. I promise you. The problem is that if we give in, yes, we stop it quickly, albeit temporarily. If we don't give in, everyone around us suffers. The solution: to leave the store immediately, after warning the toddler that we will if the behavior doesn't stop. Is this always possible? Almost. The good news is that we only have to do this once if we're lucky.

What does this have to do with gratitude? Stay with me here. More experienced parents have two choices: tell the upset child they can't have whatever the object of their tantrum is, and if they don't stop, you will both be exiting the store promptly. (I've done this.) The other choice is to tell them no, but they do have a choice about which fruit you'll buy, and then walk them over to the fruit aisle and let them pick. This also works like a charm. Why? Because now they are distracted. Their mind has something else to focus on. They can concentrate on which fruit looks and tastes good, what they will eat with it when they get home, etc. Now they're grateful they get to choose something delicious.

This seems like a parenting trick, but what you're really modeling is how to concentrate on abundance, instead of lack. You, because you're such a great parent, are showing them and talking to them about what they **can** have, instead of what they **can't** have. I think we can all agree that this is genius. What you're really doing is teaching them to change their mindset, which, on second thought, is one of the most genius things a parent can teach their child!

Gratitude is about switching your mindset from one of lack to one of abundance. Your mindset is the key to having what you want. Focusing on gratitude gets you there quicker. Like we discussed earlier in this chapter, what we focus on expands, and focusing on what we can't have will only make us want it more and feel the lack more. Remembering that we do have choices, and focusing on those choices, will not only make us feel better, but it also will help us see that the universe is actually very abundant. There is plenty of ice cream to go around, but concentrating on it because we can't have it is only going to make us want it more.

The abundance mindset, the one that comes when we practice gratitude regularly, teaches us to focus on what we can have, rather than what we can't have. Eating more ice cream won't get us to our goal of losing weight; however, thinking about all of the healthy options we do have not only helps us see what can take the place of ice cream, but it opens our mind to feel better about those options, and gets us thinking about different ways we can be healthier.

See what gratitude can do? It can help you lose weight. Isn't that awesome?

And ultimately, because we are grateful for all the choices we have, our mind becomes more open to even more choices. Honestly, thinking about everything you can have is much more fun, and the result is that it's easier to stick with your plan to eat healthier. See what gratitude can do? It can help you lose weight. Isn't that awesome?

Here are just a few more things that gratitude can help with. Several studies have shown that practicing gratitude leads to:

- Better overall physical health and better sleep
- A more optimistic outlook on life and upcoming events
- A higher likelihood that you will make progress in achieving important goals
- An increase in alertness, attention, determination, and energy
- An increase in compassionate acts and a sense of being connected to others
- Enhanced empathy
- Reduced aggression

- Improved self esteem
- Better mental health

https://www.psychologytoday.com/blog/what-mentally-strong-people-dont-do/201504/7-scientifically-proven-benefits-gratitude:

Although being grateful all day and any time of day is powerful in itself, it's especially powerful to practice gratitude at the beginning of your day when you first wake up and at the end of your day before you go to sleep. Before falling asleep, you're giving your brain and subconscious all sorts of good stuff to ruminate about. The morning practice is significant because starting your day this way, before you put anything else into your mind, sets the tone for the rest of the day.

Think about it. If you woke up thinking about everything you had to do, everything you didn't get done yesterday, all of the things you dread, or even what you can't have to eat because you're on that annoying diet, how do you think you're going to feel? Like jumping out of bed and getting to all those dreaded tasks? Nope! If, instead, you woke up immediately starting to think about how lucky you were to even wake up, in a nice warm bed, to sunshine and birds chirping, don't you think you'd be more excited about waking up? Of course, you would!

Alternatively, practicing gratitude before you go to sleep is impactful because, as you're sleeping, what you think about right before you fall asleep seeps into your subconscious mind, so you can "think" about it and process it all night long. Your subconscious goes to work and helps you digest these thoughts as you fall into a deep sleep, and helps you create more of the same. (Incidentally, this is why it's horrible to watch the news before bed.)

Do you think your brain and body would function better if you thought about negative things before you fell into a deep slumber or if you were thinking about all of the good things in your life? You guessed it! Appreciating what you have will help your subconscious mind process other ways to get more of those things you are so deeply grateful for. It sounds like magic, but it's simply using your brilliant brain and oh-so-powerfully beautiful mind to help you manifest more things to be grateful for.

> Appreciating what you have will help your subconscious mind process other ways to get more of those things you are so deeply grateful for.

I, for one (and I'm sure I'm not alone), find it much more appealing to think about having a life filled with all the people and things I truly desire and appreciate. As many of the superhero movies have taught us, and so many more types of inspirational movies have shown us, we are all truly powerful, if we only believe it. Use this power for good and gratitude and see your life change!

In addition to the morning and the evening gratitude rituals, here are some other ways to practice gratitude:

- Throughout the day, notice simple things, and express your gratitude silently to yourself or aloud
- Do it every day; gratitude requires practice
- Turn a negative into a positive
- Give at least one compliment daily (directly or as general appreciation)
- In any good or especially bad situation, ask yourself:
  o What can I learn? What will I be grateful for later?
- Vow to not complain, criticize, or gossip for a week
- Express genuine happiness to hear from/see people
- Join a cause that is important to you (donate money/time/ talent)
- Say what you want, not what you don't want
- Thank people directly (science proves you'll feel better)

One way to cultivate more gratitude, at work or at home, is to start a Gratitude Jar. Anonymously write what you're grateful for on a slip of paper and add these gratitude statements to the jar. Randomly pull out a statement for inspiration and a little joy. Go check out what you have written, whenever you need a lift.

Another idea for practicing gratitude at work (or home), or remotely, is to organize a gratitude program, where you would submit what you're grateful for via email or through a survey to one central person who can consolidate all of the sentiments anonymously and post them on a website or in a newsletter, or share them daily in a 'Daily Gratitude Email' for your coworkers to read and enjoy. Think about how you'd feel if when you open up an email - instead of reading about a problem, something you forgot, or a task you need to complete - you got to read about the things that people in your company (or family) are grateful for. Would you be smiling when you were done with that? I certainly would be.

If you're a parent trying to figure out how to teach gratitude to your kids, one of the easiest ways is to model it. Whenever your kids, no matter how old or young, are complaining to you about something that they can't have or wish they had, you can point out to them how lucky they are to have…fill in the blank. This will probably annoy them at first, and they'll have a tendency to say, "Yeah, but…."

It's your job to guide them back to the truth about having so much to be grateful for. It's about distracting them (just like in the grocery store) and pointing out the positive things they can focus on. I'm not saying this is easy. And it takes consistency; remember, it's a practice. You are showing your kids how to think about things differently. Just as you need to practice gratitude daily yourself, you need to show your kids how to do it daily. And they learn from watching you, and by your consistent, subtle reminders.

I have done this with our kids for their entire lives. Even before I began my regular gratitude practice, I would say, "Wow, look at that sunset." Or "check out how clear the sky is tonight!," "I am so glad it's sunny today." Or "I just love how bright it is outside today." This is not complicated to do, but it is something that you have to model every day if you want your children to really embrace it. It gets easier the more you do it. Eventually it won't feel like a practice but a habit. But be authentic. Kids (like everyone else) know when you're faking it. If you are not sincerely happy about something, don't pretend that you are. Instead, find something else you can be grateful for. For example, if it's raining outside and you are pissed it's not sunny again, you can say, "If we didn't have rain, flowers wouldn't be able to grow, so I'm grateful to have rain so I can see the beautiful flowers in the Spring."

Before you know it, you'll find your kids doing the same thing. I see and hear it every day from our boys. They don't complain that much, and if they do, they'll follow the complaint with something they are grateful for. And similarly, almost every time I hear them say something negative, they almost immediately say something positive. That's not an accident. It's what we've been practicing our entire parenting life. And because we knew it was important to model this, our children are modeling it for other people. How cool is that? It's very rewarding to see this insight and practice coming from your children. I have witnessed this time and time again with our boys over the years, and I can't even begin to describe how happy it makes me.

I'm sure you won't be surprised to learn that this practice will permeate into everything you're doing throughout the day-at work, at home, with your family and friends.

I'm sure you won't be surprised to learn that this practice will permeate into everything you're doing throughout the day-at work, at home, with your family and friends. You'll be seeking out the positive constantly. Although this may be annoying to some people, don't stop doing it. I'm not saying to immediately spout out what is great about someone getting diagnosed with an illness. Obviously, there's a time and a place to be sympathetic. What you can do instead is ask them about the resources they have, offer to help them with something specific you can do, talk about the ways they can feel better, etc. It's okay to recognize a problem but put your attention and energy on positive solutions. At the end of the day, we human beings cannot think of two things simultaneously. Our brains are not wired that way. No matter how smart or savvy we are, we just cannot.

So, if someone told you that they just got laid off or they may be getting a divorce, instead of asking them what they're grateful for, or worse, *telling* them what they should be grateful for, maybe you could simply ask them what sort of help they have available to them. Or ask them what sort of help they need from you. Then you can brainstorm ways to make them feel better. If you have had a similar experience, you can share what you did to make yourself feel better. This way, you're helping them shift their mindset from something that's devastating, to something that could be helpful. And as soon as your mind (and theirs) begins to do that, it starts thinking of more of the same (more helpful things to focus on).

This is similar to when you start thinking about how sucky something is, then you share your thoughts with someone who already has a negative attitude. They then add a few more negative complaints about their life or circumstances or job, and you add a few more things that are sucky, etc. Do either of you feel better when you're done sharing? No! You (and they) do not! That's because now you're both thinking about things you don't like, things that annoy you, things that make you sad. And you are in this loop that makes you feel like crap. And when you're feeling like crap, do you think you're going to have a bunch of positive, new ideas about how you can make something better? Nope.

But when you are thinking about what you are grateful for, and can be grateful for, like having good health insurance, access to good doctors, and a supportive family, etc., then you're more likely to continue to focus on those positive things, and your brain tries to find more of those types of solutions. Your mind can't do this when it's in a state of negativity. And, because you can't think of two things at the same time, if you are thinking something is bad, what's the next thought you're likely to have? Yep, something else that is crappy.

If you're going to use all that incredible power of your mind, why not use it on something that is going to make your life and your existence simply better? Practicing gratitude daily will get you into this mindset and habit more easily. Eventually, it will be your automatic setting, instead of something you have to work at and remember. The more you can practice this habit, the more likely you'll be to find the positive solution or bright side quicker. It's an amazing thing! And all you need is your mind.

As I write this in 2020, we're in the middle of a worldwide pandemic. Because that word is rarely used in our everyday lives, I wanted to be sure I was using it correctly. The word pandemic means "disease or contagion," and sadly, that word has become part of our everyday vocabulary now. You hear it at work, in stores, on the news, with strangers, and with friends. Frankly, it's almost all anyone can talk about. This is understandable.

> But what we are all slowly learning is to be grateful for all of the good things we do have and for all of the choices we still can make.

We're scared, we're anxious, and most of us have never been through anything like this. This is uncharted territory, and it is frightening. But what we are all slowly learning is to be grateful for all of the good things we do have and for all of the choices we still can make:

what to eat, where to shop for our food, which restaurant to order takeout or delivery from…these are all choices we still get to make.

- No, we can't go to school, but at least we can still learn online.
- No, we can't meet our friends for lunch, but we can all get on the phone and chat with each other and laugh about silly things for a few minutes.
- No, we can't go to our favorite mall and peruse the clothing; but we have the internet, and we can order online and get items delivered to our front doorstep - within a day, even!
- No, maybe we can't go to the health club or to a sporting event, but we can walk outside and enjoy the fresh air. We can meet new neighbors we've never even spoken to, who've had cabin fever for weeks, and who are now coming out of the house because there's no place else to go!

What else can we do to show gratitude? We can consider new ways to relate and connect to people. I'm guessing that before all of this began, a lot of us were taking for granted the fact that we could just go out whenever we wanted, hop in our car or onto the train, and simply choose where to eat, get coffee, etc. I know I was. But now, we find ourselves in a new normal. We must plan our trips to the grocery store. We must have hand sanitizer, wipes, gloves, and a mask on hand, depending on where we're going. And if we don't have the necessary gear, we cannot enter the store to procure the items we need. **What about this should we be grateful for?**

- Do we have plenty of open stores with products we need to buy for our homes and our families? Thankfully, yes.
- Do we have a plethora of websites available where we can buy those items and get them shipped to our homes within a few days, sometimes even a few hours? Thankfully, yes.

- Do we have planes, trains, and automobiles to deliver those products to our front doorstep? Thankfully, yes.
- Do we have healthy, selfless people to drive and fly those planes, trains, and automobiles? Thankfully, yes.
- Do we have beautiful, noble, committed human beings that go to work every day to take care of us when we're ill and sacrifice their health to bring us back to ours? Thankfully, yes.
- And on and on.

You can see where I'm going with all of this. If you think you need to stretch your imagination to find things to be grateful for, it doesn't take much stretching. It's all there. We're just not used to having to think about everything that goes into getting what we need to survive. We aren't accustomed to teaching our kids about these things. We aren't in the habit of sharing why we're so fortunate and helping each other see these

> If you think you need to stretch your imagination to find things to be grateful for, it doesn't take much stretching.

treasures. Now we've been forced to. And even though it's not fun to consider that we have all these restrictions, if we want to stay sane, we must consider them, then consider something else.

Gratitude comes in many flavors: big, small, silly, monumental. When I'm practicing gratitude, I usually conjure up small, seemingly insignificant things, like a cool room, nice sheets, and a comfortable bed. I don't often think about all the really big things I'm grateful for. Why is that, I wonder?

Maybe it's because the big things (i.e., health, shelter, work), seem like milestones I made happen or earned, and once earned, they're out of my head. But shouldn't I be just as grateful, maybe even more so, for all of those big things? I think maybe so. So, I will begin to incorporate those more into my practice, mainly so I can be reminded of how far I've come, and what I'm capable of creating. It seems so obvious to me now that I should give them at least the same weight as the other multitude of blessings to be grateful for. And so I will. The more often I can bring these events into my consciousness and feel so very grateful for them, the more my heart and energy expand, and consequently, the more of these same events I will draw into my experiences. Of course!

As Tony Robbins proclaims, "Life is happening for us, not to us." The problems we're experiencing every day are not necessarily things to lament. "Can you believe what just happened to me?" "You're never going to guess what so and so did to me." "Now guess what's happening?" These are just a few examples of thoughts so many of us have on a daily basis. We want the world to know that we're victims of someone or something, that an injustice has occurred that we need others to concur with.

What if we were actually grateful for these experiences, thinking instead that something, no matter how good OR bad, **is happening** *for* **us**. Our brains would shift into coming up with solutions, about positive reasons, about a better outlook. And then guess what would happen next? We'd be shifting our vibration, and we'd be in a positive state of mind, instead of going down that rabbit hole of thinking, "woe is me." Which, by the way, never leads to positivity and solutions. This is a habit we can easily maintain. It's uncomfortable at first, but like any habit we have, it's there because we practiced it. We can stop ourselves when we automatically react and, instead, pause. We can pause and wonder how this might be happening **for us** (I just accidentally typed "to us").

Dr. Joe Dispenza has written and studied neuroscience and epigenetics for years, and is a thought leader in this realm. In 2016, he conducted a study at one of his workshops. In summary, at the beginning of the workshop, he tested participants' levels of IgA, a protein in their blood that decreased when cortisol increased (stress levels). (Stay with me here.) Then he had them practice gratitude for 10 minutes, three times a day for the remainder of the three-day workshop. At the end of the workshop, these same levels were tested again. The result? The participants' IgA had increased 50%, just three days later. Simply by practicing gratitude and thinking about things that brought them joy, they changed their body chemistry! Think about that for a moment! **The cells in their bodies changed!**

It's the same concept as the placebo effect. One group of patients are given a sugar pill with no known medical effects, while another group are given the actual drug to combat their "fill in the blank" illness. Those patients who take the placebo will feel the same effects (and sometimes better) than those who take the real drug. Why? Because their brains are **concentrating on the benefits they'll experience** (or are told they will experience) and their body is responding in kind. There are numerous studies documenting this. This is not an accident: Our brains are immensely powerful. We cannot begin to fathom their power. Gratitude's power is profound. Gratitude turns what we have into enough! https://blog.drjoedispenza.com/blog/health/the-power-of-gratitude

Gratitude turns what we have into enough!

I'd like to leave you with these beautiful quotes about gratitude:

"As we express our gratitude, we must never forget that the highest appreciation is not to utter words, but to live by them." John F. Kennedy

"Be thankful for what you have; you'll end up having more. If you concentrate on what you don't have, you will never, ever have enough." Oprah Winfrey

Gratitude is the secret we can practice any time, anywhere. At work, at home and every moment in between. It doesn't cost us a penny. It brings us joy, reminds us how fortunate we are, and allows us to create more abundance. We cannot build a life of peace, possibilities, and perspective without it. Just start. Today. Now.

8

. . . . .

Manifesting

(Wait until you see how powerful you are)

Everything is energy! Every single **THING**! What do I mean
by this? Every single thing, person, or object you can think
of is made up of energy. Really! Like, scientifically speaking,
not just woo-woo energy. Atoms are filled with energy and they
make up everything we see. And it's the energy inside things and
people that gives them power. It's not the other substances.

Don't believe me? In a remarkably interesting book about
energy, *Breaking the Habit of Being Yourself*, Dr. Joe Dispenza
explains that we humans are made up of **99.99999 % energy, and
only .00001% matter**! (It's not just Joe who writes about this!)
If we're almost completely made of energy, how can we not feel
it? More importantly, why should you care about this? Because
it affects your experiences, your decisions, your ability to sense
things, even your instinct to turn one way down a street, instead
of the other. You should care because everything you do involves
energy, and if you pay attention, ***really*** start paying attention, you
will be inspired by how much power you have!

How do I know this? First, because I've read a ton of books
about it from very educated people (scientists and doctors, even).
I've listened to podcasts, attended hundreds of workshops and

conferences, and had a million conversations about energy. Unfortunately, we're not taught about this in school. I say 'unfortunately' because, if we were taught about this concept in school, when we were younger, we could be guiding, shaping, and creating the lives we want, SO MUCH SOONER than we actually do.

> We could be guiding, shaping, and creating the lives we want, SO MUCH SOONER than we actually do.

If we had been taught in elementary school even fundamental ideas about energy and our lives (not just about the atom), it would be second nature to create the life we want, instead of having our youth think that they have to go to school, work hard, pay their dues, and then finally, maybe, they can have success (I'm not saying these concepts aren't important). If working hard were the only prerequisite to having a successful life and getting everything you want, every hard-working, industrious, minimum-wage employee would eventually have financial success, just because they worked hard. Think about that for a minute—every person who works hard, busting their ass hauling wood, cleaning buildings, watching kids, etc., the people in the grind every day, struggling to make ends meet, would have awesome financial success. I'm revealing (for myself as much as for you), it isn't all about just working hard. It never was.

Luckily, because I've been reading and learning so much about manifesting, I have been doing my own experiments. And I have some stories (and proof), to share with you. The year I turned 48, I wanted a new job. I had been thinking about it for months. Why? In my current role at that time, although I had freedom, autonomy, worked from home, and really liked my boss, I wanted to do more. More what? More delivering workshops on personal and professional development. In addition to my current responsibilities, I had been running a new program at work, one that I created, presenting workshops to help employees (my coworkers) feel more connected.

Our company was global. Each person on my team lived in a different city, or state, or in a different country. I would be on a conference call with seven people, and they'd be in several different countries. This is not an exaggeration. It was very cool, but also strange. We couldn't really get to know one another, make small talk, or relate to one another on any kind of personal level. We'd join the call and get right down to business. (In theory, I agree with this "get right down to business" approach, but if you're never connecting in even the slightest personal way, it's very tough to build rapport and relationships.)

I was struggling to feel connected to any of my co-workers, so I created a monthly program to share and discuss information on topics that anyone, anywhere, could relate to. Each month, I would deliver this program to a maxed-out audience, and eventually, every month would be the same result. People wanted to hear more about these topics, to connect with others, and to do it at work! (You can read more about this experience in my chapter about connections.)

Although this program was a smashing success, it was also a struggle to accomplish this in addition to my current responsibilities. My boss was happy to have me work on this program, but it needed to be on the side, after I completed all my regular work tasks. No problem! I was happy to do that. But once I delivered the first workshop and saw all the people joining from all over the world, and felt that energy... I was hooked. I knew I needed to figure out a way to get paid to do this every day! (And incidentally, I said those exact words to my best friend on the same day I realized this.)

And so off I went, looking for a role in which I could do just that!

At first, I tried to move to another department at my current company. I really liked the company I worked for and what they stood for. They had a great reputation, and many different departments. There were a few openings, but nothing that fit my aspirations. Then I advocated for a hybrid role, where I devoted part of my time to these types of programs, and the other part to my current responsibilities. After several months of trying to work this out, it turned out not to be feasible. Ultimately, I couldn't have what I envisioned. So, my job hunt started.

As I searched for a role in which my sole responsibility was to create and deliver these workshops, I was excited to find a company who wanted these programs and was willing to pay me to implement them. It wasn't happening as fast as I wanted it to, but at the same time, I was strengthening all the other areas of my life, so I would be able to benefit from good energy all around.

My birthday was approaching, so I thought I'd use this birthday to deliver 48 random acts of kindness. What a great way to celebrate—give back and create some good experiences for myself and others. I started with small things. I left flowers at my neighbors' doors. I brought candy to the local crossing guard who was always smiling. I wrote thank-you notes to friends. I left a Starbucks gift card at the fire department's door, and so on. At the coffee shop counter, I'd randomly pay for the order of the person behind me. It was so fun to come up with new ideas. I started this several weeks before my birthday so that, on my birthday, I would be celebrating 48 random acts of kindness, instead of wondering what gifts I'd be receiving.

Completing 48 random acts of kindness was also a nice distraction from my job search. Although I had some interviews and was gaining momentum in my search, I was growing impatient. As they always say, when you're feeling down, go do something for someone else. So that's what I did! Forty-eight is a large number for this type of activity. Coming up with fun things to do was easy, at first. Then came the planning and executing of each idea. I didn't initially consider all of this and how time consuming it would be, but I kept on because it was delightful creating these experiences.

At this same time, while planning all of these random acts for others, I enrolled in an awesome wellness workshop for myself and was able to really hone in on exactly what I wanted in my next role, as well as for the rest of my career—a role where I could use my strengths and my gifts every day and be paid well to do it. I traveled to Miami for this workshop, staying in a beautiful hotel on the beach, and ultimately, leaving with a road map to continue my career journey. It was a blissful three days.

> As they always say, when you're feeling down, go do something for someone else.

After this trip, and as I was completing my 48 random acts, I was also progressing in the interview process with one of my potential job opportunities. Initially, I didn't think this role was senior enough, but after talking to my potential new boss, I realized that it was exactly what I wanted, and I even recommended changing the job title to be more in line with the responsibilities. This role was definitely more of a leadership role, and not just about executing programs at the instruction of others.

As I continued to interview with additional people at the company, I became more and more excited about this role, and really wanted the offer. At last, I was in the final stages of the selection process, with only a few other candidates, and the company was hoping to make a decision very soon. My birthday was fast approaching, and I was hoping I could celebrate it with my dream job offer.

I planned my exit at my current job and waited for the new company's final decision. I knew if I weren't offered this role, it would mean that there was another even better role for me around the corner. I finished my random acts of kindness, kept working, walking, and hoping. And then it happened. On my 48th birthday, I received the call. It was from my new boss, offering me the job. She told me I should be expecting an offer letter with all of the details in a few hours, but she wanted to extend the offer to me verbally and fill me in on the details! I couldn't believe it! Here it was, my birthday, I was getting the job offer I really wanted, at an office just 4 miles from my house, and I was being offered more money than I'd ever been paid for any role. Wow! What a way to celebrate my birthday.

After I had considered the offer, including the benefits and all of the other details, I really wanted to negotiate a slightly higher salary. This is always tricky. I say that to the women reading this— it's just not as tricky, typically, for men. There's plenty of research regarding this subject of job hunting and negotiation. In summary, men don't hesitate to negotiate; it's just not a second thought for them. Women hem and haw about it, wondering whether they've earned the right to ask for more money. We're less likely to be confident about our skills and what we can offer, assuming we should just be grateful for the offer. Newsflash: Hiring managers are expecting us to negotiate! When we don't negotiate, we actually make them second guess their decision a little, wondering why we don't think we're worth more. (I actually had a hiring manager tell me this!)

> When we don't negotiate, we actually make them second guess their decision a little, wondering why we don't think we're worth more.

In the end, I had obtained my next role that would align with my strengths and mission, and all because I determined very clearly one day that I needed to find a way to make money every day performing in this type of role. It would take me about eight months, but I did it! And all along, giving back to others and believing it was coming. Then doing the work. Eight months is better than never!

I told you this works, didn't I? And if you don't yet believe me, here's another personal example of manifesting:

In 2018, I signed up for an event that I wanted to attend that would be held in 2019 in New York. The cost of the event was $5000, but if you paid in full before the event, the cost was discounted to $4700. I was determined to go to this event, and have it paid in full before I attended the first session. That gave me ten months to pay it off. So, I made the commitment and paid $470 per month and did just that. I knew I needed to be at this event. I knew it was going to be life changing. I knew I would meet amazing people. It was. I did. (There are many experiences I could write about from this life-changing event, and I likely will in my future writing endeavors.)

Fast forward to the following spring when the event was taking place. I had to be in New York for three weekends. This would require airfare and hotel for each weekend. I was able to book my first weekend using airline miles and hotel points, spending just a minimal amount of money. For the second weekend, I could only attend the event for one day, so I needed just one night at a hotel. Summertime in New York is expensive, and because of the cost, I hesitated to book a hotel. I again booked my flight with airline miles, but still didn't have a place to stay.

While in New York for the first weekend in April, I met a wonderful woman on the first day of the event. We had lunch and hung out periodically over the course of that weekend. As we were chatting about the May event we'd both be attending, I told her that I hadn't booked my hotel yet, and really only needed a room for a few hours. She immediately offered to let me stay at her home in Brooklyn, because she was going to be at her beach house that weekend and her place would be vacant. I would just need to feed her cat! I was shocked, and grateful. Here I was, a mere stranger just hours earlier, and now this lovely lady is offering to have me stay for free at her place in New York. Now I wouldn't need to spend the extra money for just a few hours in a hotel. Voila! Accommodations taken care of.

When I returned home after that first weekend in New York, I wanted to capitalize on the momentum I was feeling. I was experiencing so much great energy about what I wanted to create in my life, and although I liked my new job well enough, the position was eventually not everything leadership had proposed it to be, and that nagging feeling that I still wanted to deliver these awesome workshops, connecting people, was still in the back of my mind. I knew when I returned from the New York events, that I was going to finally put the pieces in place to make this happen, once and for all.

Instead of trying to find a job where I could fit my workshops in, I was going to CREATE a job where my workshops were the highlight. This was a huge epiphany for me. I wasn't finding exactly what I wanted "out there" in the corporate world, because I needed to create it. OKAY! Now I had the clarity, so it was time to make it happen.

> Instead of trying to find a job where I could fit my workshops in, I was going to CREATE a job where my workshops were the highlight.

One of the first things I did was to reach out to the other women from the conference who lived in my area. I knew that, in order to keep the momentum going, I needed to be around and connected to that same energy I felt in New York, and these like-minded women would be a huge support. I emailed them, explaining that I wanted to connect with them, stay engaged, and possibly get together, so we could all capitalize on this awesome energy. To my great delight, I was met with the same excitement. They all wanted the same thing and were thrilled to be able to connect with each other locally. Now, over a year and a half later, we are good friends, supporting and loving each other, connecting regularly, and have become a part of each other's lives. All because I had an idea, and I sent an email. (How's that for manifesting more of this great energy?!)

Then May rolled around. Following that first conference week-end in April, although I was plugging along, paying off that conference each month, due to other family commitments, bills, and trips we had planned, we had accumulated more debt. This was typical as we managed our goals along with our dreams, and the ever-changing unexpected events and glitches that come up in daily family life. I know we can all relate. It seems like whenever you have "extra" money, an appliance finally breaks and there goes your "extra."

I was investing the maximum allowed in my 401K at work, saving more than we'd ever saved, even though I had taken a pay cut at my latest job (more on that later). I was almost done paying off my conference, and we had an additional $5,200 in debt that also needed to be paid off. I casually said to my husband out loud one day in the spring, "I want this $5,200 paid off by December," which at that time was seven months away. He agreed we could do it, and that was the end of the conversation. We didn't discuss what to do or how to do it. We spoke about it once, and that was it. That was it!

A few weeks later, on the morning of Mother's Day (in May), we decided to all go see a movie. We've never done that on Mother's Day; not that I can recall. When we arrived at home, our oldest son took our old Honda Civic to drop off his girlfriend, who had attended the movie with us. Maybe 20 minutes later, he was just a few blocks from returning home when he was hit by an oncoming car. The other driver (at fault) just barreled through the four-stop-sign intersection and hit the passenger side door of our Honda Civic with a ton of force. So much force that the passenger's seat was cracked from the door smashing it. The air bags exploded, too. It was frightening to think that our son's girlfriend had been in that very seat just 10 minutes before. Our son wasn't injured. He was a little in shock. He was apologetic. He was confused about how this could have happened. But everyone was safe. The other driver had a young kid in his car, and neither of them was injured either. That was definitely a surprise, and a relief.

But our car was undrivable, so we took it to the repair shop for an estimate. The damage was too great, and the car was totaled. This was also unfortunate, because this was the car that our son was planning to drive when he moved to Florida. Incidentally, I'd never wanted him to take this car on the long road trip to Florida; it was 10 years old, and it made me nervous, given the number of miles he'd be driving it. I just didn't like the idea of it. My motherly instincts were setting in. I said out loud, "I don't feel comfortable with him driving that car to Florida".

To recap: It's May, our son just totaled our car that he had been planning to take to his new home and job in Florida, and we owed $5200 dollars on our credit card that I had just told my husband I wanted to pay off. It would seem like these events were unrelated, until the estimate from our insurance company came back. Since our car was totaled, they'd be giving us a lump sum of money.

Once I saw the connection to what I requested—and was so clear about wanting—and getting it done, I was amazed at how easy it was.

Can you guess how much? The lump sum of money our insurance company would be giving us was $5,200! Once I saw the amount from the insurance company, I knew immediately that we were meant to be using that money for our debt. That debt would be paid way before the December timeframe I had initially requested.

Once I saw the connection to what I requested—and was so clear about wanting—and getting it done, I was amazed at how easy it was. All along, we hadn't really planned to give one of our cars to our son. It was something my husband had been thinking about offering him to help him on his move and new life in Florida. It was something he mentioned in passing one night.

We could have given him the money that we received for our totaled car, but then he'd be buying a used car that would likely have its own issues; or he'd be using it toward the purchase of a new car and then still have a monthly car payment. The idea of giving him the money felt a lot different than that of giving him the car, especially once I saw that the money totaled $5,200. There was no doubt it was meant for our debt.

Our son did the grown-up thing (and the thing we parents are meant to model) and decided that he'd get to Florida and buy his own car there. And he did just that. Within a month from that car accident, he had graduated from college, found an apartment in Florida, bought a new car in Florida, and started his new job. And we paid off $5,200 in debt. Wow, what a difference one month can make!

Need more proof? Here's yet another manifesting story.

I woke up one morning in January, just a few weeks away from my husband's 50th birthday. This was the year we were planning to possibly go to Italy, combining a business trip with a long-awaited vacation. I wanted to have a party for my husband, but he wasn't really keen on celebrating that way. Since there wouldn't be the expense of a big party, I thought we'd save our money for the trip to Italy in the fall, celebrating his birthday and our 24th wedding anniversary at the same time.

This January morning, I awoke with a noticeably clear thought: we were not going to Italy this year. I don't know why I had that thought so vividly. I'm not sure why we ever have these lucid thoughts that usually happen on a whim in no particularly sensible order. But that was my thought. Italy wasn't going to happen in 2020. The clarity of this statement came to me as soon as I woke up. This is the power of our subconscious mind and our intuition. Listen to it when it comes. (If I hadn't listened, I would have been planning a trip to France and Italy in the fall of 2020, when no one would be traveling, instead of planning and taking the trip I'm about to share with you.)

Just a few weeks before this clear thought popped into my mind, our good friends had moved to Puerto Rico and were welcoming visitors. We dreamt of visiting them there, but given work, time off, the other trips we had planned, along with regular life expenses, fitting in this trip wasn't likely. Until that day I woke up in January.

Since I knew intuitively Italy was off the table, on this day I decided to start looking into a trip to Puerto Rico and what it would entail. I've always been good at quickly assessing whether indeed something is possible or not. If it was $1,000 per person to get a flight there, not possible. If it was $200, maybe possible. I need to know up front whether something is out of reach, then I can get it out of my mind. If something is possible (and usually it is), then my brain can start making room for exactly how it will be possible.

> If something is possible (and usually it is), then my brain can start making room for exactly how it will be possible.

This is something I've been able to do since I was a kid. When I had questions about how something worked, how it came to be, or what it was about, my dad used to say, "Let's go look it up in the encyclopedia." For those of you younger folks reading this today, that's the equivalent of saying, "Let's

Google it." My dad would have loved this concept! Before he died, I urged him to let us purchase a laptop for him so he could look up any and everything to his heart's content. Just typing in a question, then having the answer within a few seconds is mind-boggling for those of us who grew up without the world wide web. My dad never quite embraced this concept and was resistant to using a computer. I hate that he missed out on this. (Carpe diem, people!)

So, off I went to "Google" it. As I began to research, I looked to see when my credit card payment was due and realized I had earned almost 80,000 points on my credit card in the past year. Hmmm. I hadn't spent that much on this card. In a typical month there would only be a few hundred dollars on this card, and if we were on a trip, maybe over a thousand dollars until we returned and paid it. I'm still not sure how I earned these points, but it was likely due to a business trip I took in August the year before that I used this card to pay for and was reimbursed. (Side note: there are perks to NOT having a corporate card.)

I wondered what my points were worth in regard to travel and incentives. This card was fairly new, and I didn't even know what these points could be redeemed for; I hadn't had it long enough to research these options. As luck would have it, these 75,000 points were worth quite a bit when used for travel. With this card, a cardholder could convert their points into a certain amount of cash. But, if the points were redeemed for travel (i.e., flight, hotel, or car), then these points would be worth much more. Simply put, I could cash in these points and have a nice lump sum of cash, or I could turn them in for travel and have 25% more money to spend! Hmmm. Can you see where I'm going with this?

After my initial assessment of these points, I realized I had almost $1000 to use for travel and was excited to start looking into the cost of flying to Puerto Rico. Due to spring break occurring in

March or April, it turns out that flying in February is a few hundred dollars cheaper, and that worked very well with our schedules. Once I began researching flights, I discovered that many of the airlines stopped in Florida on the way to Puerto Rico. Our son was living near Fort Lauderdale—wouldn't it be cool if we could stop and see him on the way to Puerto Rico? Of course, it would! My husband would especially love that surprise.

As I reviewed flights, I found we had enough points to fly to Florida, stay for a few days, then fly out of Miami to Puerto Rico. We could then take a non-stop return flight from Puerto Rico back to Chicago! We had enough points to cover these flights, and with an additional $135 total, we would have the entire trip paid for! Wait a minute—I could spend just $135 dollars and book three flights for each of us? I'm sure you don't have to guess what I did next.

I called our friends in Puerto Rico and asked which dates worked for them for our visit. We agreed on the last week of February. I called our son in Florida to be sure that weekend worked for him as well. All set! I called my mother-in-law to be sure she could stay with our teenager for the week. Done! And then I booked the flights. We were going to Florida to visit our son for two days, spend a day in Miami, and then on to Puerto Rico for five days. And another bonus: I had enough hotel points from other travels to stay at a beautiful hotel right on the beach for our day in Miami, with a pool to lounge at all day while we enjoyed the ocean view, and then fly out first thing the next morning to be in Puerto Rico by noon the next day. In total, with the flights for all these legs of travel (six for both of us) and the hotel stays, we'd only pay about $200 out of pocket.

All of this research and planning happened in just a few hours. All because I woke up one morning and simply had the epiphany/ clarity that Italy wasn't a reality, and maybe there was something better in store for us. When we make a decision, it's amazing how many doors open for us. Those doors may not be wide open; it may just be a crack. It may be a window that is open now. There may be a window

> When we make a decision, it's amazing how many doors open for us.

you didn't notice before. The point is that the universe guides you, once you decide. Sometimes it is as simple as saying, "I don't want this." Or ,"I want that." Actually, it's almost always as simple as saying it. When you get clear, everything else gets clear. Your path becomes apparent. Things you hadn't considered suddenly pop into your mind. And off you go, making it happen.

Manifesting can occur in any aspect of your life. As a family, when our boys were younger, we often watched Food Network shows; in our house, it was either sports, food shows, or documentaries. We always struggled to find shows our family could all watch together, without inappropriate messages or values that didn't sync up with our own.

One of those shows was *Restaurant Impossible*. This show focuses on helping restaurants revitalize their businesses and get back to the heart of why they ventured down this path to begin with. Robert Irvine is the host, and he has a team of people working to redesign each restaurant and bring it back to life. One of the designers is Taniya Nayak.

Every time we'd watch the shows, we all squealed with delight when Taniya would appear, because she was our favorite. She exudes light and love. Her eyes sparkle, and she simply loves what she does. My husband and I could always see it. Our boys could always feel it. They'd ask me, "Mom, what is it about

> That's what it looks like to love your work and that is what we should all strive for!

her?" And I would proclaim, "She loves what she does! That's what it looks like to love your work and that is what we should all strive for!" They agreed. (Thank you, Taniya, for showing the world this virtue!)

Fast forward to January 2020. Since my podcast, *Peace and Possibilities* focuses on people who love the work they do, I am always looking for people who fit that bill. My only prerequisite is that you have to love what you do and want to talk about it. I want people to hear these stories and see themselves finding work they love, making a difference in this world, and being happier and more peaceful along the way. Taniya Nayak is the epitome of this!

One day, my husband said, "Honey, you should get her on your podcast." I thought, "I should. I will." It was that simple. I decided that I would, and off I went figuring out how. I looked up her website, emailed any address I could find, called and left messages, and finally, I was connected to her assistant. What made it possible?

During my research, I had emailed Taniya, explaining my podcast and why I would be honored to have her as a guest. The email finally made its way to her, and she accepted with open arms. Why? Because what I wrote was real and true. I told her how we thought she lit up the screen every time we saw her on the show, and that I wanted my boys to absorb that and strive for that essence in everything they pursued. She was touched, and she agreed to be on my podcast. We finally scheduled it in March 2020. She was the last podcast I released before we all knew what "Corona" would mean in 2020. Sound too easy? I agree. But it is many times, and very often, just that easy.

Manifesting isn't just wishing, it's believing.

I wrote myself this check in September 2019 and dated it for September 2020.

This check was written to manifest the success of my business and bring in $250,000 of income to our family. I wrote this at the same time I was launching my business. I wrote this to prove to myself (and my 17-year-old son) that this manifesting stuff really works. Is it magic? No. Well, kind of.

You can't just put your thoughts or desires out there, then sit at home and be depressed because you don't have them. You can't just do every negative thing you can imagine and have that money

> I wrote this to prove to myself (and my 17-year-old son) that this manifesting stuff really works.

drop in your lap. But you can say or write or dream about what you want, then go about your days, weeks, and months thinking positively about what you want, and *feeling* what it would be like to get it. And then taking advantage of opportunities to make these things happen, embracing any little thing that points you in the right direction.

I committed to having that money in a year. I felt what it would be like to have that amount of money flow into our lives. I expected to have it. I was excited to have it. And I worked at other things to get me to a place where I could really see what it would be like to have it.

Then, guess what happened? It was July 2020, and I didn't have that money yet. I was two months away from "accepting" this money into our lives, with no real potential (yet) from my business to have clients pay this amount of money for my services. I had recently quit my well-paying job to focus on my business full time. I was working daily to write, connect with potential clients, and promote my podcast. But I still hadn't sold my first program.

Then, in mid-July, something unexpected happened. On my daily walks, I began to notice how quickly the homes in our neighborhood were selling. Houses put up for sale were selling in days, and sometimes not even going on the market officially before offers were coming in. I wondered what our house would sell for, and whether indeed we'd sell quickly. After a brief assessment of the inventory on the market, I could see that our house, though built in 1950, was modern and updated like no other on our block.

We'd originally considered selling our home in early 2021, after our youngest son was settled in at college. But now that real estate was so hot, maybe this would indeed be the right time. So, we inquired. In just a few days, we discovered that our house could be listed for at least $250,000 in the current market. Hmm... that's interesting. Maybe we should put it on the market and see what happens, we thought. Our real estate agent recommended finishing a few projects we had started, and then we listed it. Who knows – let's see what happens, he said.

We listed it a few weeks later, and lo and behold, it sold within 24 hours. And guess how much it sold for? You wouldn't be crazy to guess $250,000. But you'd be wrong. We listed it for more than that, knowing how updated and turnkey it was compared to the recent houses that sold in our neighborhood. We listed it for $268,000 and sold it for $264,000. And guess when we had that money? Yep. We closed and had over $260,000 of money flowing to us on September 16, 2020. Just four days before I dated that check!

Another interesting coincidence? The original request from the buyers was to close on the sale of our house on August 28, but due to paperwork and

> It's ultimately the power of believing that gets you exactly what you expect.

the busy real estate market with appointments overwhelming them, the closing was pushed back a few times, and eventually was moved to September. Of course, it was. Wasn't that my original request when I wrote that check for $250,000 just one year ago? Yes! There we were in September 2020, and just like I wrote and expected, that money flowed to us. Was it how I expected? No, not exactly. Was it better? Yes.

That's the power of manifesting, my friends. It's real. Don't believe me, just try. And mainly, just believe. It's ultimately the power of believing that gets you exactly what you expect. We definitely have the power to control our thoughts and manifest what we desire. We do!

I'm going to leave you with some very important words from the book, **Think and Grow Rich,** by Napoleon Hill:

> *"He should have told us that the ether in which this little earth floats, in which we move and have our being, is a form of energy moving at an inconceivably high rate of vibration, and that the ether is filled with a form of universal power that ADAPTS itself to the nature of the thoughts we hold in our minds; and INFLUENCES us, in natural ways, to transmute our thoughts into their physical equivalent.*
>
> *If the poet had told us of this great truth, we would know WHY IT IS that we are the Masters of our Fate, the Captains of our Souls. HE should have told us, with great emphasis, that this power makes no attempt to discriminate between destructive*

thoughts and constructive thoughts, that it will urge us to translate into physical reality thoughts of poverty, just as quickly as it will influence us to act upon thoughts of riches.

He should have told us, too, that our brains become magnetized with the dominating thoughts that we hold in our minds, and, by means with which no man is familiar, these "magnets" attract to us the forces, the people, the circumstances of life which harmonize with the nature of our dominating thoughts."

Take that in for a minute. No matter what you focus your energy on, that's what you create.

And one final influential quote, from Regena Thomashauer, author, leader and a brilliant woman, whom I've had the great pleasure of working with:

"Your dreams are not too big for you. You would not have them if they were not just the right size and shape for the individual you are. They are blueprints of your fulfillment. Everything you want you can have. Don't worry about money – the price tag will get in the way only if you let it. If you could trust your dreams half as much as you doubt them, you would get everything you want."

Manifesting is the ultimate secret to living the life you want. You can create anything you imagine, but you have to know what you desire. You have to be specific and intentional. This takes reflection, but thankfully, once you figure it out, it only takes a second to make the statement. And then you let the universe get busy making it happen. Go ahead, manifest your dreams. Our planet needs them!

Conclusion

I grew up not quite knowing what I wanted and looking in countless places to help me figure it out. I was always searching for people and things that were going to help me learn and grow. I know we all have our own path. We need to figure many things out for ourselves.

But wouldn't it be great if we didn't have to do it all on our own? What if each of us had that special fairy godmother or godfather that we could go to every time we had a question or a problem? For a lot of you, I'm guessing this is your parents. I'm hopeful it's your parents. You are blessed if it's your parents. For many of you, I'm presuming this is your spouse or your friends. If so, then good for you for choosing well. I'm happy to say, I did too.

I wrote this book because growing up, I didn't have enough of these people in my life. I always wanted more wisdom and guidance. I didn't see a plethora of people around me to offer it, so I found it myself. It took years. I'm still accumulating it.

So, for all of you who are in that boat with me, I offer you my fairy-godmother wisdom, gleaned along my never-ending journey. I hope this book has enough insight for you to start living the life you've always dreamed of. I hope this book is like an old friend or mentor that you can relate to and remember when you need a boost or a reminder of just how powerful you are.

You have so much wisdom inside of you. Seeking it elsewhere is sensible, but not necessarily required. Use these eight secrets every day and do whatever it takes to accumulate your own wisdom. And never stop learning or growing!

Peace,
Julie

Review Inquiry

Hey, it's Julie here.

I hope you've enjoyed the book, finding it both useful and fun. I have a favor to ask you.

Would you consider giving it a rating wherever you bought the book? Online book stores are more likely to promote a book when they feel good about its content, and reader reviews are a great barometer for a book's quality.

So please go to the website of wherever you bought the book, search for my name and the book title, and leave a review. If able, perhaps consider adding a picture of you holding the book. That increases the likelihood your review will be accepted!

Many thanks in advance,

Julie Bruns

Will You Share the Love?

Get this book for a friend, associate or family member!

If you have found this book valuable and know others who would find it useful, consider buying them a copy as a gift. Special bulk discounts are available if you would like your whole team or organization to benefit from reading this. Just contact julie@2possibilityandbeyond. com or go to https://2possibilityandbeyond.com.

For weekly inspiration, sign up for Julie's newsletter:

https://2possibilityandbeyond.com/sign-up-for-inspiration

Would You Like Julie Bruns to Speak at Your Organization?

Book JULIE Now!

Julie Bruns accepts a limited number of speaking and training engagements each year and would be thrilled to engage with the awesome people at your company. To learn how you can bring her message to your organization, email julie@2possibilityandbeyond.com.

Resources

The Peace and Possibilities Podcast

For a plethora of stories on resilience, connection, possibilities, manifesting, and more from wonderful people who have been there and done that, check out my podcast. Then subscribe and leave us a 5-star review on whichever platform you listen.

The Peace & Possibilities Podcast
http://peace-and-possibilities-podcast.libsyn.com/

The Peace & Possibilities Podcast on Apple Podcasts:
https://podcasts.apple.com/us/podcast/peace-and-possibilities/id1485218863

The Peace & Possibilities Podcast YouTube Channel
https://www.youtube.com/channel/UCI03e0XfY3Nbvzfk4WmmKpQ/videos

The Peace & Possibilities Podcast on Spotify
https://open.spotify.com/show/2TlhrteFzGVVq5oeFC7wVn

Want to be my guest?

If you love what you do, and you'd like to be a guest on my podcast, reach out! The possibilities are endless.

Want to meditate and manifest more?

If you're interested in starting a meditation practice, and after learning more, why wouldn't you be, check out the Breethe App - it's simple, affordable, and so easy to use.
Start now!
https://main.breethe.com/share

To incorporate more mindfulness, gratitude, and manifestation, check out this daily priming exercise from Tony Robbins: https://www.instagram.com/tv/B_LB7VtnoBZ/?utm_source=ig_web_button_share_sheet

Books:

Breaking The Habit of Being Yourself: How to Lose Your Mind and Create a New One by Dr. Joe Dispenza

Real Happiness at Work by Sharon Salzburg

Want to feel more gratitude and create more joy?

Book

Joy, Inc.: How We Built a Workplace People Love by Richard Sheridan, CEO and Chief Storyteller

Article
*https://www.huffingtonpost.com/guy-kawasaki/
workplace-joy_b_5034427.html*

Article
*http://www.ascd.org/publications/educational-leadership/sept08/
vol66/num01/Joy-in-School.aspx*

Article
*https://www.huffingtonpost.com/carolyn-rubenstein/
how-to-find-joy-at-work_b_695159.html*

Article
*https://www.inc.com/jessica-stillman/this-is-best-way-to-practic
e-gratitude-this-thanksgiving-and-any-day-science-says.html*

Article
http://renewyourmind.co.nz/30-day-gratitude-challenge/

Want to build more resilience?

Books
Everything is Figureoutable by Marie Forleo
Resilience by Eric Greitens
The Gifts of Imperfection by Brenee Brown

Article
https://www.verywellmind.com/what-is-resilience-2795059

Article
https://positivepsychology.com/what-is-resilience/

About the Author

Julie Bruns grew up as 1 of 11 children in the suburbs of Chicago. She is 1 of 8 girls and the 7th oldest child. (That is one of the most frequently asked questions she gets when she tells people how many siblings she has.)

As a talkative and curious child, she loved to draw, play her trombone, and be as social as possible. She was always wondering about the possibilities of her life: what she could be, what she could have, and where she could go. After many years of searching and asking questions, she is excited to tell you what she has learned.

After graduating with a BS in Marketing and Economics, and a Masters' degree in Teaching, she has spent her corporate career as a software trainer and leadership development trainer, teaching clients and companies all over the world, in industries including healthcare, IT, consulting, travel, and environmental health and safety.

Her podcast, "The Peace and Possibilities Podcast" is another platform that shares stories from successful, happy people who love the work they do, and can help you learn just how to get there sooner. Through her podcast, Julie has interviewed CEOs, entrepreneurs, college students, TV personalities, and authors from diverse backgrounds. If you want more inspiration, listen in or check out her weekly blog. You'll find a never-ending stream of awesome people, great insights and illuminating ideas she is excited to share.

Life is an amazing experience, if we could just remember that we are here to thrive and be happy. She is not saying you don't have to work hard. Just keep these 8 secrets in mind as you go along on your journey and you will be on your way to a happier, more peaceful and content life, where you can experience all the wonderful things the world has to offer. To possibility and beyond!

Julie lives with her husband in beautiful downtown Chicago, and can be reached at: https://2possibilityandbeyond.com/ and julie@2possibilityandbeyond.com

CPSIA information can be obtained
at www.ICGtesting.com
Printed in the USA
BVHW050247120321
602277BV00019B/853/J